101 Allergy-Free Desserts

Frances Sheridan Goulart

A Wallaby Book
Published by Simon & Schuster, Inc.
New York

To my supporting cast—Ron, Sean, Steffan . . .
Esme Carroll, of course . . .
and my supportive editors, Gene Brissie and Melissa Newman

Copyright © 1983 by Frances Sheridan Goulart

Published by Wallaby Books
A Division of Simon & Schuster, Inc.
Simon & Schuster Building
1230 Avenue of the Americas
New York, New York 10020

Designed by Judy Allan (The Designing Woman)

WALLABY and colophon are registered trademarks of Simon & Schuster, Inc.

First Wallaby Books printing August 1983
10 9 8 7 6 5 4 3 2 1

Manufactured in the United States of America
Printed and bound by Fairfield Graphics

Library of Congress Cataloging in Publication Data
Goulart, Frances Sheridan.
   101 allergy-free desserts.

   "A Wallaby book."
   Includes bibliographical references and index.
   1. Food allergy—Diet therapy—Recipes.   2. Desserts.
I. Title.   II. Title: One hundred one allergy-free
desserts.
RC596.G68 1983   641.8′6   83-4728
ISBN: 0-671-45785-3

Contents

FOREWORD

When Frances honored me by asking that I write the fore-word to this food allergy-oriented dessert book, I thought it would be helpful to review a number of well-known cook-books to refresh my memory regarding dessert recipes. I spent about five pleasant hours in "library research" on this subject. I read a famous cookie recipe book, the dessert sections of *The Settlement Cook Book*, and Craig Claiborne's latest *New York Times* cookbook.

The desserts that I "investigated" included cookies, cakes, cake and pie fillings, puddings, soufflés, ice cream, candy, doughnuts, fritters, blintzes, crepes, waffles, and I quickly became reacquainted with the fundamental composition of des-serts in general.

Desserts are prepared from mixtures of commonly eaten foods, and this same group of foods is also present in our daily menu. Many of these common foods are in forms that are easily recognizable. However, some "dessert foods" may be overlooked because they have been disguised in one way or another and are present as "hidden foods." Desserts are a problem for food-allergic people because most of the ingredients in their favorite desserts are foods that are eaten very often—perhaps several times a day. And it is very difficult to avoid these dietary offenders unless one makes a special effort to do so. Just about everyone—including you—is exposed to these foods. In allergy-prone individuals, a heavy exposure to a dietary item is a major factor in the development of an important illness-inducing food allergy or a state of allergic addiction to a number of frequently consumed foods. If one is not a careful observer, the order in which foods are placed in lists of ingredients will almost hide the fact that the majority of dessert recipes share many foods in common.

Food allergy is the unsuspected and overlooked cause of numerous forms of serious physical and mental disorders that affect millions of people throughout the world. These disorders include a variety of disabling and painful chronic internal allergic conditions like arthritis, colitis, and migraine—as well as some forms of headache. They seriously affect the quality of life of millions of food-sensitive individuals whose reactions to foods include fatigue, depression, anxiety, nervousness, restlessness, irritability, dizziness, lightheadedness, visual blurring, short attention span, impaired concentration, poor memory, itching, indigestion, and urinary tract disorders.

Many food-allergic children are hyperactive and learning disabled; or they may be emotionally unstable; some are unable to control their urinary bladders. Other food-sensitive youngsters may suffer from headaches, stomach aches and/or "growing pains." Some cases of schizophrenia manifest their mental symptoms because food intolerance has caused reactions in their very sensitive brain tissues.

Unsuspected, unrecognized, and misdiagnosed allergic and ecologic ailments of body and mind often have profound effects on the physical and mental health of those who are afflicted. The patients' condition—as well as the dietary and environmental measures that are required to control these disorders—also affect the lives of members of their families in many significant ways. It is not unusual for some of the necessary restrictions on the overall family life-style to be the source of considerable resentment that may surface from time to time. Unfortunately, certain aspects of case management may remain a continuous source of irritation to some individuals.

Unfortunately, most of the individuals who are victims of food-induced allergic illnesses are misdiagnosed and incorrectly treated. This situation exists because the fundamental nature of disorders resulting from food allergies is not understood by most physicians. Modern medicine is at least twenty years behind the times with respect to the important breakthroughs and progress in the closely related fields of allergy and clinical ecology—as well as in nutrition.

Another important aspect of the overall problem is that most of today's medical care is rendered by the drug-oriented and psychiatrically oriented physicians in mainstream medicine. They usually concentrate their professional energies on obtaining relief for their patients' presenting symptoms because they do not realize that the symptoms they are treating are the manifestations of internal forms of unrecognized food allergy, sensitivity to environmental allergens and chemical agents, and biochemical-nutritional disorders. They do not seek out the underlying causes of these ailments to determine which illness-evoking factors can be avoided or controlled in many instances. Many incorrectly diagnosed patients are mistakenly referred to psychiatrists for treatment of nonexsistent "neurotic" or "psychosomatic" conditions. We are confronted with a tragic and completely avoidable situation that is widespread in the practice of modern medicine.

There is good news for most of us who have food allergies. Between 50 and 75 percent of our *food allergies are not necessarily permanent*. They do not have to remain with us, creating difficulties with meal planning and causing health problems for the rest of our lives. We can eliminate our sensitivity to many food allergens by controlling our exposure to them. This even includes those very potent food offenders that are responsible for many serious chronic disorders. They are the kinds of illness that often put large numbers of foodallergy victims (and chemically sensitive individuals) into both general and mental hospitals.

For many food-allergic people, it's simply a matter of having a suitable respite from those dietary offenders, which will provide an adequate biologic rest period. In addition, it is necessary for them to pay careful attention to their individualized problems of food dosage. How much of a given food can be tolerated at a single feeding, and how often can it be eaten without causing allergic reactions? Special attention must also be given to ingested chemical agents and pollutants of the indoor and outdoor air because the food-allergic individual is much more likely to react to minor and borderline foods when undergoing chemical stresses.

If foods that presently act as allergic offenders are eliminated for six weeks to three months, there is an excellent chance that currently active allergic sensitivity to these foods will disappear and be replaced by *a state of tolerance.* The state of tolerance to a former offending food or group of foods can last indefinitely if these foods are not eaten too often after tolerance has been regained. Restricting the intake of a food allergen that one has "recovered" from by eating it only once (in any form) every five to seven days or longer will preserve the fragile state of tolerance to foods that have been responsible for important allergic disorders of body and mind.

For many people, *food addiction* is the most important—but not widely known—aspect of food-related illness. In many ways, food addiction is similar to narcotic addiction and alcoholism. The major features of food addiction are the unwanted appearance of very distressing food-withdrawal symptoms, and the almost irresistible demands of the food-addicted individual's body for the relief that can be obtained by eating the addicting food that is responsible for the withdrawal reaction. This explains a number of familiar problems including the frustrating and previously misunderstood actions of the food-addicted compulsive eater who has taken a "diet pill" but still eats on schedule at mealtime. He or she has taken a very effective appetite-depressing medication and is not the least bit hungry. But, despite the lack of hunger, he positively must eat in order to be physically and/or mentally comfortable. Here is urgent, physiologically driven, uncontrollabe eating in the total absence of appetite. Here is an irresistible biologic need to eat—not an emotionally based act of psychological self-gratification by a deprived individual who does not receive the affection that he longs for.

Addiction also explains food binges and cravings; "late-for-meals" symptoms that are relieved after eating the missed meals; food-relieved middle-of-the-night symptoms affecting many areas of the body (itching, asthma, nightmares, insomnia, indigestion, headache, etc,); midnight raids on the refrigerator; symptoms present on awakening in the morning that clear after the addicting food is consumed for breakfast (a mid-morning person) or at lunch (an afternoon person).

Substances derived from foods and beverages enter the body, are acted upon in the stomach and upper intestine, are digested and then pass through the intestinal walls into the circulatory system. They soon reach every part of the body—including the brain with its very rich blood supply. (The bloodstream, containing food-derived materials from the intestines, transports them to all potential sites of reaction throughout the entire system.)

Symptoms due to allergic reactions can occur anywhere and in any combination, depending on the location of what I call a person's *Biologic Weak Spots*. Each food-allergic individual has his or her particular group of allergic reaction characteristic symptoms that will occur during an allergic reaction. I have named these individualized combinations of symptoms *Patient-Specific Syndromes*. This explains how a person with food allergies may manifest the same group of symptoms over and over again.

Often, such a patient may find that he is in a difficult situation with his physician if the doctor is not familiar with the clinical picture that is characteristic of internal forms of food allergies and food addiction. The patient who has this very common type of allergic-ecologic illness, who knows that he always becomes ill "the same way each time," cannot convince the doctor that his bodywide symptoms, physical and mental, represent a genuine disorder. The patient may "look too good to have all those symptoms," and the physician does not know of any disease entity that is characterized by the patient's "peculiar" assortment of seemingly unrelated symptoms. That famous "It's all in your head" or "Stress" diagnosis is made. Tempers have flared as repeated observations of intelligent patients meet the stone wall of medical training that is totally lacking an ecologic perspective. At this distressing and unnecessary state of affairs, it is not unusual for the services of a psychiatrist to be recommended—often with considerable emphasis.

I conclude this introduction to food—related physical and mental disorders with the hope that I have clearly described for each reader an important and fascinating area of medicine. I hope that you are now aware of the basic facts regarding allergy to commonly eaten foods—and this certainly includes desserts which are combinations of major food offenders.

Food allergy is a very frequent cause of major health problems that affect the health and happiness of millions of children and adults. It is for all of them that Frances wrote this excellent book.

Marshall Mandell, M.D.
Medical Director, The New England Foundation
for Allergic & Environmental Diseases

Introduction: Are You Allergic to Dessert?

When things are getting worse, send chocolate, goes the joke. But if you're allergic to chocolate and to the ingredients such as corn, sugar, or milk that usually accompany it, it's no joke.

A food allergy can strike at any organ or part of the body. It can upset digestion, clog the nose, or inflame the brain. According to the *Journal of Learning Disabilities,* in a five-year study of 182 hyperactive children, 75 percent of them were found eating foods that either caused or complicated their problem. Twenty-eight were allergic to chocolate, 38 to milk, 30 to corn, 20 to eggs, and 15 to wheat. And a similar study conducted by Dr. Doris J. Rapp, an allergist at the Meyer Memorial Hospital in Buffalo, New York, indicated that of the hyperactive children tested 70 percent showed evidence of having allergies. Fifty percent of these children showed improvement in their hyperactivity in *one week or less* on a diet that excluded milk, eggs, wheat, corn, sugar, cocoa, and food coloring.

A common ingredient like chocolate, which is a close rela-
tive of the kola nut, from which Coke and the popular food
additive gum karaya are made, can cause anything from
sneezing to schizophrenia. So can a "good" food, such as milk.
Milk and other dairy products have been linked to arthritis,
heart disease, and dental cavities, and it is estimated that up
to one-half the world's population is allergic to some degree to
dairy products, causing such disorders as eczema, recurrent
ear infections, nasal congestion, abdominal bloating, irritability, asthma, fatigue, and joint pains. Also characteristic tip-offs
of symptoms of milk allergy that often vanish when milk is
discontinued, says psychologist Robert Forman, are a bron-
chial-like cough, sinusitis, post nasal drip, and enlarged glands
in the neck.

As for corn? Corn products "can cause a mild stomach upset in one person and throw another person into a deep depression for two days," reports one researcher, in the study
Orthomolecular Nutrition.

And wheat may be even worse. According to Dr. A. Alvarez
of the Mayo Clinic, whole wheat bread can pass through the
whole of the small intestine without being digested at all.
Wheat seems to interfere with the absorption of other foods,
in much the same way salt does. In fact, "wheat is the greatest
culprit among foods in connection with the causing of allergic
effects," agrees Dr. Albert H. Rowe, world-renowned expert
in the field of bronchial asthma and a leader in allergy research. In tests on hundreds of allergy sufferers, Dr. Rowe
found wheat to be the cause of over one-third of their allergies. Wheat is particularly detrimental in the presence of
eczemas, hives, and migraines. As a combination, one that
occurs often in the more than 400 desserts we eat each year,
whether in the form of store-bought Twinkies or homemade
bread pudding, milk, wheat, and corn with or without chocolate can be a triple threat.

"Dairy and cereal or grain products are the two types of
foods most frequently found to cause severe cerebral reactions. Milk products, wheat, and corn can lead to psychotic

symptoms both in 'normal' people and in patients diagnosed as being emotionally disturbed," says nutritionist Dr. Carlton Fredericks in his book *Psycho-Nutrition*. Fredericks relates the case of a boy susceptible to wheat allergies, whose reactions included hyperactivity, delusions, behavioral problems, and learning disabilities. All of these "disappeared when wheat products were removed from his diet. . . . In another patient eating corn or any grain product—wheat, rye, oats, or rice— led to fatigue, coughing, and depression."

Even if you aren't bothered by *these* offenders when the dessert cart rolls around, that *still* leaves other food offenders—sugar and spice, yeast, citrus, nuts, soybeans and eggs, and food additives to name a few—that could get you if you don't watch out.

What is a food allergy? What allows some of us to eat, drink, and make merry with mousses and 3 Musketeers bars while the rest of us react? In brief, say allergists of the classical school, allergy is an overreaction of the body's immune defense system to a specific foreign material that would produce no effects in a nonsensitive person. Allergic reactions result from the activity of a specific class of immunologic substance called immunoglobulin E. Allergic reactions can range from mild to serious: from a skin rash to a loss of blood pressure and state of shock. Susceptibility to allergies often seems to be inherited. It is speculated that each allergic person may have a unique "allergic fingerprint," a group of substances to which that individual may react.

How many of us are allergic? One hundred million may even be a conservative estimate with our numbers growing due to other factors that contribute to allergic disease, such as polluted water, dirty air, and occupational stress, says clinical ecologist Marshall Mandell.

If the mechanism of allergic reaction is not simple, neither are the causes. Allergies appear to be inherited. A genetic lack of essential digestive enzymes can cause problems. People affected in this way may not be able to digest certain foods. This can cause a deficiency of certain essential nutrients. No matter how much the person eats, his or her body doesn't get enough nutrition from the food it digests. These nutritional deficiencies can then lead to changes in behavior and mood.

Allergies may develop if the body becomes "sensitized" through eating large quantities of one particular food. This problem has an additional twist. A person can eat so much of one food that he or she actually becomes addicted to it. A dependency develops and the sufferer craves large quantities of the food because it gives a temporary emotional high. This often occurs with foods, such as milk, that may be consumed one to several times each day. You can also inherit a certain chemical makeup that rejects some foods.

Almost any food can cause an allergic reaction (though the least allergy-provoking substances appear to be lamb, rice, squash, pineapple, and sweet potato). You can be allergic to one food, to many foods, or to a general food "type" such as cooked foods or canned foods. You could be allergic to a food because it is treated with preservatives or insecticides.

Regardless of what triggers an allergy, it is the body's natural immune response system that leads to the symptoms. The body's antibodies see the problem food as a foreign substance. This triggers an antigen-antibody response which in turn triggers many physical changes throughout the body. These physical changes cause the allergy victim to suffer.

Symptoms can occur immediately, or hours later. They can last one, two, or even ten days. One important factor, say researchers, is the length of time the food remains in your system (the time taken for digestion and elimination) and the time required for the body's natural antibodies to react with the food allergen.

Your problem is twofold if you have both an allergy *and* a sweet tooth. A real "junk food" dessert may contain all the top allergens, but for that matter a good "healthy" dessert like Mom's apple pie may have them, too. What to do? Don't desert dessert. But getting rid of the not-so-good-for-you goodies on the menu isn't such a bad idea. In fact, it *could* change your life. According to Dr. Mandell, if you eliminate food offenders you may increase your tolerance of airborne allergens, such as pollens, molds, house dust, and animal danders, as well as environmental chemicals. This benefit occurs because the allergic stress caused by foods has been minimized, thereby allowing you to better cope with other factors.

What if you don't know whether you're allergic or not? Check out your suspicions with this simple test suggested by Dr. Mandell:

1. Avoid the most common offending foods (which are probably the top allergens discussed in chapter 1) and see how you feel in a few days or a week.
2. Make a list of the foods you eat *infrequently* (about once every five days). Eat these in place of the "offending" foods on a daily basis. You will probably eliminate most allergic offenders this way and feel better.
3. Under no circumstances should you eat *any* food that you love, crave, or eat on binges. Any food that creates a sense of well-being is off limits. Such responses to food are signs of food addiction, one of the most common factors in food allergy.

Better yet, go to a good allergist. Organizations such as HEAL and the Allergy Information Association (see Appendix C, p. 180) can tell you who's who and what is where. After all, why face a lifetime of behavior-disorienting desserts? Or even a lifetime of runny noses every time you have a piece of pie?

Meanwhile, no matter what your gotta-have favorite is, or what your don't-touch-it intolerance may be, there is a way to have your allergen-free cake or pudding and eat it, too. Read on.

NOTE: There is no food that isn't an allergen for somebody somewhere. Even pure spring water bothers a few of us. But some foods are statistically worse than others, while some are statistically safer than others—and those are the ones to be discussed in the following chapters.

I. The Top Allergens

Sugar

The average American consumes over 2 pounds of refined sugar a week. As a nation, Americans eat 28 billion pounds of sugar each year. Individually, that works out to 160 grams or 20 teaspoons a day. (A single Coke contains 9 teaspoons of sugar.)

That's a lot. It's too much for anybody, *more* than too much if you're allergic to sugars, the most important and recurrent ingredient in dessert. There are, in fact, dozens of sugars commonly used in commercial baking, dessert making, and candy manufacturing these days. And they're all bad for you in varying degrees, twice as bad if you are allergic. Some are worse than others. Refined sugar and corn syrup cause worse reactions than unrefined honey, for example.

Sugar in any form is a stress food, says Natalie Golos,

coauthor of *Coping with Your Allergies,* and raw sugar is loaded with bacteria. What's more, she adds, according to pediatric allergist Dr. Joseph Morgan there would probably be no food allergies at all if we started infants on rotary diversified diets, omitting sugar and additives. (A *rotary diversified diet* is one which rotates and varies the foods since allergies and addictions are caused by the frequency with which a food is eaten.)

Why? Because the faster a food is absorbed from the intestinal tract, the more likely it is to produce an allergy/addiction response. And right behind alcohol for speedy absorption are the refined carbohydrates like white sugar and corn syrup.

And if you are allergic to the petrochemical hydrocarbons, the problem is even worse. Because along with several certified food colors and lots of nonfoods like room fresheners, candles and perfumes, white refined sugar is a petroleum by-product.

From a chemical standpoint, there are two kinds of sugar—monosaccharides and disaccharides. Monosaccharides are the simplest sugars, and the only kind that can be absorbed across the intestinal wall. They include glucose, mannose, fructose, and galactose. Disaccharides—sucrose, lactose, and maltose—are made from two monosaccharides joined together. Disaccharides must be broken into their components before they can be absorbed (just as with all absorbable carbohydrates)—a process that takes place in a wink.

And this is where the trouble starts. Sugar enters the bloodstream so quickly that it causes the blood-glucose level to surge. When blood sugar rises, specialized cells in the pancreas secrete more insulin which in turn causes body cells to store sugar, and muscle and liver cells store it as glycogen, the emergency fuel. Other cells store it as fat. Quick blood-glucose elevations can form a good deal of fat.

When faced with a large influx of sugar, the body tends to overreact and overproduce insulin. When insulin pumps too much glucose out of the blood and into the cells, low blood sugar, or hypoglycemia, results. Fifty to 90 percent of the population, says Dr. Harvey Ross, president of the International College of Applied Nutrition, may suffer from this syndrome whose symptoms include fatigue, nervousness, and a constant craving for sweets. Long-range symptoms encompass depression to mental confusion to schizophrenia.

In humans, sugar has been observed to alter blood chemistry, interfere with protein utilization, and like coffee, step up gastric juice activity to a health hazardous level.

How does sugar do all this dirty work? According to Dr. John Yudkin, "The effects of sugar in disease can occur in three different ways: 1) by pushing out other foods from the diet; 2) by being taken in addition to other foods; and 3) by the particular properties of sucrose." One of those properties is sugar's ability to make people allergically ill. As Britain's Surgeon-Captain Peter T. L. Cleave points out in his book *The Saccharine Disease*, "Sugar is much more dangerous than white flour, because it is eight times more concentrated."

Sugar comes in so many forms you may not recognize the enemy without a scorecard. It is found under one name or another in 80 to 90 percent of our food supply—from wine to "unsweetened" dry cereals to infant formulas, so scrutinize labels. The basic ingredient may be sugar beet, sugarcane, or corn but all of the following are forms of refined sugar: brown sugar, cane syrup, dextrin, refined sugar syrup or refiners' sirup, dried corn syrup, corn sweetener, glucose, glucose solids, golden sugar or golden syrup, maltose, grape sugar or dextrose, invert sugar or invert sugar syrup, levulose, liquid brown sugar, turbinado sugar.

Here are a few facts about the three refined sweeteners we use the most (information provided by Vermont Country Maple, Jericho Center, VT 05465):

Sugarcane. Harvested stalks° are shredded and crushed to

°Paradoxically, sugarcane, which is not very sweet, is rich in minerals, trace minerals, and vitamins, and is not a cariogenic food but becomes a hazard only after it is "purified." The refining process increases sweetness and removes the nutritional elements needed for your system to metabolize sugar. As a result, sugar easily creates nutritional deficiencies.

produce a juice that is clarified with various chemicals, usually either calcium hydroxide (slaked lime) or trisodium phosphate (detergent phosphate). This removes impurities, such as fiber, fat, wax, dirt, chlorophyll, etcetera. It also removes many of the minerals normally present. The juice is then evaporated, crystallized, and centrifuged to produce a raw sugar, not to be confused with so-called raw sugar sold as raw, because true raw sugar is not clean enough for human consumption, and its sale is illegal.

Raw sugar reaches the refinery, is sometimes chemically clarified again, and then decolorized with activated charcoal. This removes what minerals remain. Refining consists of successive evaporations and crystallizations, called "strikes," to yield the various sugars. The first strike yields white sugar; the second, light brown sugar; the third, dark brown sugar with molasses as a residue. The darker sugars are more processed than white sugar, which is produced first.

Beet sugar is produced in essentially the same fashion and, in fact, the two are sold interchangeably although labels are not required to carry this information.

Corn products. Cornstarch yields corn syrup, which is primarily glucose after a series of treatments with enzymes and acid hydrolysis. Additional enzymatic treatment of corn syrup produces high fructose corn syrup which is about half glucose and half fructose. Pure fructose is separated from the mixture and concentrated to either fructose syrup or dry fructose sugar, the two forms in which it is sold.

"The use of the term 'fruit sugar,' which is the old common name for fructose, just as 'grape sugar' is the old common name for glucose," says maple syrup processor Lyman Jenkins, "is very misleading as to the sugar's actual source. Fructose is *not* natural by any stretch of the imagination; it is manufactured from cornstarch."

How about the so-called natural sweeteners?

Pure maple syrup and honey are both produced by essentially the same process, diluting the raw material gathered from the plant and removing the excess water. To make maple syrup, the sap of the maple tree is gathered and excess water is removed by boiling. In the case of honey, the excess water is removed from the flower nectar by air evaporation in the beehive. It takes about forty gallons of maple sap to make a gallon of maple syrup, compared to only about two gallons of flower nectar to make a gallon of honey.

And a new process now makes pure maple syrup available in granular form. Three steps (evaporation, rapid stirring, and air drying of the crystals) turn the syrup into a completely dry powder with all the nutrients and flavor of the original maple syrup retained.

Both honey and maple syrup are mineral rich. The calcium content of maple syrup, for instance, is comparable to that of whole milk. The following table compares the average mineral contents of maple syrup and honey.

Average Mineral Contents of Liquid Natural Sweeteners per 100 Grams (values in mg./kg.)

	MAPLE SYRUP	HONEY
Potassium (K)	2,600	1,194
Calcium (Ca)	1,250	87
Magnesium (Mg)	186	34
Phosphorus (P)	130	47
Manganese (Mn)	110	9
Sodium (Na)	4	43

In addition, both maple syrup and honey contain small amounts of the minerals iron, zinc, and copper.

On the other hand, lots of us are allergic to honey and maple syrup, too. What else looks good? See the next chapter, p. 39.

Corn and cane sugars belong to the cereal family (see Wheat), beet sugar belongs to the goose foot family along with spinach, and maple syrup and sugar belong to the maple family. Honey, classified botanically as "miscellaneous," is without family.

Considering a so-called sugar substitute? Don't.

The field of possibilities looks larger than it actually turns out to be. All told, there are about three dozen alternatives to refined sugar if you include the miracle berry, the serendipity berry, and other yummy-sounding analogs. (Read *The Sugar Trap* by Beatrice Trum Hunter, Houghton Mifflin, 1982, for more details.)

Since many of these nonsugar sugars are still on the drawing board, the ideal substitute at present is one that's safe for diabetics and weight watchers, one that neither rots the teeth nor erodes the health, is safe for hypoglycemics, tastes great, cooks just like table sugar, and yet doesn't trigger an allergic reaction.

One that may fit the bill but isn't yet available is called "left-handed sugar" (L-sugar for short), because its molecules are arranged in the mirror image of regular "right-handed" sugar. And it passes right through the body and doesn't make you fat, says L-sugar's promoter, Gilbert V. Levin, Ph.D., president of Biospherics, Inc., in Rockville, Maryland. Levin, who has patented its use in foods, soft drinks, and drugs, hopes to have his product in mass production by 1984. But will it be hypoallergenic, too? Who knows?

Cyclamates had looked good until they were banned back in 1970 when it was found they caused bladder tumors and chromosome damage in rats.

Which leaves us with:

Saccharin. This nonnutritive sweetener, which contains no calories because it isn't absorbed by the body, has been in use for over eighty years. It is, in fact, the most widely used substitute in the world. Until recently, the only thing wrong with it was the metallic aftertaste. Now it's in danger of being removed from the market because numerous studies have shown that heavy use of saccharin causes an increased risk of cancer.

According to the National Cancer Institute, if you drink two or more eight-ounce diet sodas a day, or use six or more daily servings of saccharin, your risk of bladder cancer is increased by 60 percent. If you smoke and use saccharin, you have a higher risk of bladder cancer than nonsaccharin-using smokers. And while bladder cancer is three times more frequent in men than in women, the risk for women using saccharin or diet drinks twice or more daily increases by 60 percent.

It doesn't take much: Saccharin foes argue that even the highest level of saccharin consumption in tests was only 1/300 of the minimum reported to produce bladder tumors in rats. They also point out that there has been an increase in cancer of the bladder among diabetics who eat great quantities of saccharin and have done so for decades.

The FDA made plans to ban the use of saccharin in foods and soft drinks in 1977. When the news got out, users flooded the agency with letters requesting that Congress "save" saccharin. As a result, there is a moratorium in effect until the summer of 1983. Meanwhile, saccharin is undergoing more tests to determine if, in fact, it really is a threat to human health.

The safety of saccharin aside, it is inadvisable to use it if you are allergy prone. There are numerous cases of reactions—everything from nausea and disorientation to fits of coughing. Tenseness and anxiety are common symptoms.

Aspartame, trademarked Equal, is the newest alternative. It has been sold in Europe and throughout Canada since 1981 and has recently been approved for use in the United States. The first cold cereal to use aspartame is the Quaker Oats Company's Halfsies, now available in most supermarkets. It's the only other new sugar substitute with almost zero calories. It isn't even a carbohydrate, but is composed of two amino acids, phenylalanine and aspartic acid.

Aspartame is several times sweeter than sugar, so you use less. Aspartame looks and tastes like a powdery refined sugar, and is said to have no adverse effects on the teeth, pancreas, or blood sugar levels. What effects it may have on the allergic metabolism are yet to be disclosed.

Aspartame has drawbacks. It contains milk sugar, for example. It can be used only as a table sweetener. Cooking or baking causes its amino acids to degrade and the sweetness to dissipate. Over one hundred safety tests have been performed on the product so far, so it is FDA-approved as a sweetener in gum, cereals, beverage products, gelatins, and puddings, as well as in packets and tablet form. It is also used in some brands of diet soft drinks.

Fructose occurs naturally in all fruits and some vegetables. It is the sugar that makes fruit taste sweet, just as lactose, the sugar in milk, makes milk taste sweet. Unfortunately, the fructose sold in health food stores and supermarkets most commonly comes from cane, beet, or corn sugar that has been split into its two components through an ion exchange process.

Fructose concentrations vary from 42 to 55 percent, and the Center for Science in the Public Interest adds "that fructose is even more highly processed, and therefore *less* natural than regular sugar." Pound for pound fructose has the same caloric count as table sugar, and is about one and a half times sweeter. It is still an empty-calorie food.

One possible plus is that fructose metabolism is less dependent on insulin than refined sucrose so moderate amounts of fructose can be used by hypoglycemics and controlled diabetics[*] without bad effects. But, according to a report in the Archives of Internal Medicine, "fructose causes abnormalities in body chemistry."

Toxic effects—all coronary risk factors—have been noted when fructose in quantities well above that consumed in a normal diet were used. These included a rise in uric acid levels in the blood, elevated triglycemia levels, disturbed synthesis of liver protein, and increased production of fat in the liver. Fructose in large amounts can also cause flatulence and diarrhea.

Xylitol, sorbitol, and mannitol are all naturally occurring alcohols, not carbohydrates or proteins. They contain the same number of calories as refined sugar. Xylitol, which can be extracted from various cellulose products including wood pulp or sugar cane pulp, is similar in taste and sweetness to sucrose. Sorbitol, which is extracted from fruits including plums, cherries, and apples, and mannitol, which is found nat-

---

[*] The American Diabetes Association suggests you consult your physician before using fructose if you are diabetic.

urally in pineapples, olives, asparagus and carrots, are only 50 percent as sweet. (However, if you are allergic to these foods, you may react to these substitutes.)

All three produce diarrhea and/or abdominal cramps when consumed in large amounts. Unfortunately, xylitol has been cited for promoting urinary bladder stones and tumors in mice, and sorbitol appears to interfere with the absorption of B_{12}.

One plus to xylitol is that it does not promote tooth decay like sucrose, which is quickly metabolized by bacteria in the mouth, forming acids that cause cavities. Researchers in Finland and Norway have found this quick metabolism doesn't occur with xylitol, and it may even stimulate your saliva to fight and prevent caries.

On the other hand, according to a recent University of Pittsburgh study, mannitol and sorbitol convert into lactic acid which attacks the teeth, increasing caries. "Sugarless gum isn't sugarless," explain the university researchers. "It is sucroseless. If you look at the labels, you will see that most of them are 60 percent carbohydrates, and that can be just as bad as sugar. The bacteria which cause decay can survive and multiply on those carbohydrates."

Because xylitol, sorbitol, and mannitol do not require insulin for metabolism by the body, they are considered sugar alternatives for diabetics by some doctors. However, recent studies in Russia indicate that a high-sorbitol diet may present real problems for the diabetic because the sorbitol may accumulate in cells and disturb the nervous system, the blood vessels, and the eyes.

Although these sweeteners are widely used in products such as toothpaste or chewing gum, their safety is still in question, and all three are being evaluated by the FDA for carcinogenicity and other adverse health effects.

Milk

Dairy products have the highest consumption of any major food category—only 6 percent of Americans say they don't consume fresh milk in some form. Yogurt consumption has tripled in the last two years. Cheese consumption has doubled since 1960, and in 1982 the average American ate about twenty-two quarts of ice cream, an increase of 25 percent over 1981. However, along with wheat, milk is the country's leading allergen. Milk has been called a perfect food. But is it?

Milk is a good source of high-quality protein, carbohydrates, B vitamins, and calcium, but it's also loaded with nonessential saturated fats and cholesterol. And in various studies, cow's milk has been linked to obesity, atherosclerosis, and tooth decay. It also lacks some very important nutrients, such as vitamin C and D and iron.

As many as 20 percent of children in the country under the age of two suffer from iron-deficiency anemia, largely due to too much iron-poor milk.

According to Dr. Lawrence Naiman, chief of hematology at St. Christopher's Children's Hospital in Philadelphia, milk irritates the digestive tract, causing low-grade gastrointestinal bleeding. The amount of blood is small, but it can be enough to lower iron supplies and cause the symptoms of iron-deficiency anemia—fatigue, inattentiveness, headaches, lack of muscle tone, and pallor—especially in small children.

Milk may even be hazardous to your health. Drinking a lot of cow's milk is a bad dietary practice. "I think I could make a better case for milk being a junk food than I could for a Big Mac and an order of fries," says Dr. Nathan Smith, a professor of pediatrics at the State University of New York's Medical Center in Syracuse.

Researchers at the University of Colorado and the University of Miami Schools of Medicine have traced a form of persistent kidney disease known as nephrosis to milk allergy. Nephrosis is a disorder in which excess amounts of protein are lost from a damaged kidney into the urine, producing a lowering of the blood-protein level and causing pronounced fluid accumulations. Nephrosis can advance to renal disease and be fatal.

At the very least, milk can crowd other needed foods out of the diet and lead to an unbalanced eating pattern and all the problems that go with it.

According to Dr. Lenden H. Smith, author of *Improving Your Child's Behavior Chemistry*, dairy products are the worst allergic offenders. The lactose that appears in fresh milk undergoes a change when the milk is made into yogurt or cheese, which contain all the nutrients of milk in a more digestible form. Someone who has no lactose enzymes in his or her digestive tract can enjoy these foods, even though he or she cannot drink fresh milk.

Milk is a significant trouble maker. Why? Because milk, like wheat, is one allergen that can rarely be overcome. Even after three months of abstinence, those sensitive to milk find they are still sensitive.

Milk contains three major types of protein that are allergenic: casein, lactalbumin, and globulin. Of the three proteins, lactalbumin is the most troublesome. Casein is found in the milk from both cows and goats, but the lactalbumin in each is different. For this reason goat's milk, in some cases, is often substituted for cow's milk.

In addition, it is possible that boiling the milk can change the major proteins so that they are no longer allergenic. For example, lactalbumin and globulin are denatured by heat, but casein is not.

There's also a possibility that you may tolerate whey buttermilk, yogurt, or a low-lactose cheese such as brick, cottage cheese, Gouda, or provolone. Test yourself or have your doctor do it.

Milk allergy can cause anything from sniffles to digestive trouble to swelling of the hands, feet, and abdomen. And children who are the most sensitive may experience nasal congestion, attacks of asthma, chest infections, persistent or recurrent skin rashes, vomiting, and diarrhea. Allergy to cow's milk is more likely if someone in the family has allergies, too. Children with hay fever or asthma-afflicted parents are always good candidates.

What's the solution if you develop symptoms that are obviously related to your milk intake?

Give it up.

But don't neglect calcium from some *other* source, such as broccoli, collards and spinach, green beans, and sea vegetables—kelp and dulse, for instance. Supplements such as calcium lactate, dolomite, and bone meal solve the problem too. And don't forget Brazil nuts and almonds, both of which supply as much calcium as milk. (But see Nuts, in this chapter.)

Remember especially that giving up dairy products will not be easy. Besides avoiding butter, cheeses, ice cream, milk solids, and nonfat dry milk, look out for foods that have sodium caseinate, lactoglobulin, and lactalbumin on the labels. (These foods offer another peril for the allergic—federal law exempts the manufacturers from listing artificial color on the label.)

Milk is found in such commercial desserts as pudding, tapioca, and junket; in cocoa drinks, caramels, chocolates and fudge; in cookies, cream toppings, and frostings; and in frozen novelty desserts and sherbets.

As you can see, when it comes to products containing milk, it is a cast of thousands. For example, did you know that there's milk in chocolate syrup or Cool Whip nondairy whipped topping or Cremora nondairy creamer or Fudgsicles? If a little milk causes a lot of trouble, protect yourself by reading labels and asking questions.

If you're chemically sensitive you have one more reason to avoid milk: It often contains formaldehyde. And note that milk belongs to the bovine food family, which includes beef as well as dairy products.

Alternatives? See the next chapter.

Wheat

Wheat is our daily bread. The sweeter the better. According to the Industry and Trade Administration, an estimated $3.86 billion worth of cookies and crackers were shipped by the U.S. bakery industry in 1980—a $1.19 billion increase since 1975.

Wheat contains major nutrients. It is rich in magnesium, for example. And why is that important?

If the levels of magnesium and calcium in the blood are too low, the signals between the nerves and muscles become mixed up, resulting in twitching and tremors. Neurologic symptoms and signs are the most prominent and frequent manifestations of disturbances in the metabolism of magnesium, according to researchers. Patients who suffer from anxiety, depression, weakness, and psychosomatic disorders frequently have low levels of magnesium in their blood.

Wheat is also a major allergen. And what kind of reactions does it cause?

If your nervous system is affected, notes Lawrence E. Lamb, editor of *The Health Letter,* you could experience "changes in personality and mood, headaches, even vertigo [the illusion of motion] may occur and the allergic reaction may involve the balance canals of the ears resulting in allergic labyrinthitis. The peripheral nerves may be involved or even the nerve to the eye causing optic neuritis. . . ."

Wheat is one of the eight foods that commonly lead to hyperactive behavior in children, says Dr. William G. Crook. And a significant number of anorexia victims also suffer from an addictive allergy to wheat, reports Cheryl Hawk, D. C.

There is also a special form of wheat allergy called celiac disease in which sufferers react to the gluten protein in *all* grains, including wheat. Reactions cause abdominal distention with severe diarrhea and often hemorrhoids. Among grains, only corn and rice are gluten-free.

If your digestion is affected by wheat, notes Dr. Lamb, the allergy may cause severe swelling of the intestines which in turn causes cramping and pain. Gastroenteritis, resembling acute bacterial food poisoning, or gaseous distention with pain, nausea, vomiting, and diarrhea, is a common allergic reaction. Wheat allergy can also cause constipation and even itching of the rectum and "bilious" attacks. "Inflammation of the lining of the mouth [stomatitis], the gums [gingivitis], and even bad breath all may be caused by a food sensitivity such as wheat allergy."

Worse, wheat, if consumed often enough and long enough to become a serious allergy, can affect your ability to cope with life itself. Dr. Theron G. Randolph illustrates this point in his book, *An Alternative Approach to Allergies:*

"She [the patient] alternated between binges of eating and fasts or all-fruit diets . . . and loved bread, baked goods . . . anything with wheat in it. She had eaten wheat addictively since childhood, when her mother, who was interested in nutrition, became convinced of the virtues of whole-wheat bread. She therefore plied her daughter with large amounts of this staple. [The patient] who had a family history of alcoholism, likened herself to an alcoholic in her craving for bread."

But through the *avoidance* of wheat, Dr. Randolph concludes, the patient was able to control both her depression and her weight problem. (No wonder! A slice of bread has 60 to 80 calories, 180 if it's a bagel. One bagel does more caloric damage than a whole pound of cauliflower.)

Wheat is also one of the five food allergens that commonly causes eczema, a severe skin complaint that affects 2 million people a year.

Then, what's good about wheat? It's rich in all the B vitamins from the antistress factor, pantothenic acid (B_5), to biotin, the B vitamin that reputedly helps prevent premature hair loss. Wheat is a good source of protein, calcium, iron, and other disease-preventing trace minerals. Above all, it is a superior source of vitamin E, the antioxidant nutrient.

But if wheat's out, it's out. And out it is for millions of us. According to the Human Ecology Research Foundation, wheat is probably the number one food offender for young people (it's tied with milk).

In addition to avoidance of wheat from the obvious sources and replacing it with safer grains and foods (see chapter II, pp. 39–56), consider supplementation. According to researchers at the University of Sydney in New South Wales, tolerance for gluten can sometimes be restored if papain, the enzyme that comes from a tropical tree (the same enzyme used as a meat tenderizer) is taken regularly. A tablet of crude papain in enteric-coated tablets with every meal could get you back on the bread-and-toast track.

.   Avoiding wheat means passing up candy, Cream of Wheat, farina, graham flour, ice cream, Ovaltine, Postum and coffee extenders, or "blends," pumpernickel, rye, vitamin E (made from wheat germ oil), plus bran, buckwheat, wheat germ, wheat gluten flour, wheat starch, whole-wheat flour, white enriched flour. Other sources of wheat include MSG (not *all* MSG is wheat-based but most is). And malt and malted cereal syrup are sometimes derived from wheat.

Even if you skip a dessert dish and have a drink, instead, watch out. You get wheat in any cocktail made with whiskey, gin, ale, or beer.

Wheat belongs to the food family of cereal grains, which also includes bamboo, barley, corn, millet, oats, rice, rye, sorghum, sugarcane, triticale, and wild rice.

As you can see, wheat is not an easy ingredient to avoid, but the effort will be well worth it. See the next chapter for alternatives.

Corn

"Corn tends to be a staple in countries that have very high homicide rates, such as Latin American countries," say A. R. Mawson and psychologist K. W. Jacobs, researchers at Loyola University in New Orleans. "Corn has a much lower amount of the amino acid tryptophan—which has a calming effect on people—than many other foods."

According to Dr. R. T. Rinkel, corn is the dominant form of food allergy in North America. Why? Because surprisingly enough, it is the most commonly eaten food in North America.

And any food eaten day in and day out becomes an allergen for a large percentage of the population (coffee and milk are two examples). Corn is also a major allergen in desserts. It may, in fact, be *the* major allergen.

"Many people think they are not consuming a particular food when they are in fact having it every day," says Dr. Marshall Mandell. "You may not eat corn as a vegetable very often, yet you eat it at practically every meal in the form of corn sugar (dextrose or glucose), corn syrup, cornstarch, corn oil, or as a hidden ingredient in other foods, such as beer or whiskey."

What kind of clues can you expect if you suspect corn allergy? Asthma is common, but so is skin rash. Why? Because corn is used in soaps such as Zest, in plastic food wrap, and on the sticky side of stamps and envelopes.

It may even be a pain in the foot. Dr. Mandell writes in *Dr. Mandell's Five-Day Allergy Relief System,* "When one lady with asthma was exposed to corn extract she developed pain in her left ankle. After she removed corn in all forms from her diet, what she had considered her 'arthritis' disappeared."

According to Antigen Laboratory's nutritionist H. Buttram, corn is the most difficult food in the diet to avoid as it is found in an array of foods, which can cause minor reactions and a *continued* sensitivity to corn. Reintroducing corn to the diet can be risky unless it is preceded by a total elimination of it.

What are you missing if you drop corn from your diet?

Not that much. The protein corn contains, called zein, doesn't measure up to the protein in other grains; corn is high in fiber and carbohydrates—but so are a lot of other *less* sensitizing grains. If it's yellow corn, it supplies vitamin A, but unbalanced diets too heavy in corn can lead to niacin deficiency, even diseases such as pellagra.

But corn has a long history, and a good reputation. The American Indians revered corn. It was their dietary mainstay, after all. They roasted it right from the stalk—a method still used at cookouts. They also ate it combined with beans as succotash, or picked it green and boiled it in milk pressed from the kernels. They dried mature ears and then ground them into meal for use during cold spells. Ground corn was mixed with water and baked as the unleavened bread we still love in twentieth-century American tortillas. Plains Indians used corn silk as a "sugar," even incinerated the cob then mixed the ashes with foods made from corn to preserve minerals. So valuable were corn's medicinal properties that corn smut *(Ustilago)* earned a listing in the American pharmacopoeia as a vasoconstrictor and antihemorrhagic. Dried corn grains were beaten into a poultice for sores and ulcers; fresh meal was dissolved in water and drunk to prevent dysentery; a liquid extract from corn silk (the stigmas of the female flowers) was a remedy for bladder and urinary dysfunction. Corn oil was used for everything from hay fever to migraine headaches and dandruff. There was even a custom among early settlers of placing corn on the grave to feed the deceased's soul.

As multipurpose as corn is, if it's got to go, it's got to go. (See chapter II, pp. 46–48, for what you can put in its place.)

Corn belongs to the cereal/grain food family that also includes bamboo, barley, millet, oats, rice, rye, sorghum, sugarcane, wheat, wild rice, and triticale (a wheat-rye hybrid).

Corn is found in the following: bleached flour, some baking powders and yeasts, beers, chocolate drink mixes, breads and pastries, soft drinks, dry cereal such as Cheerios, instant coffee and tea, deep-fat frying mixtures, fructose, sugar substitutes, vanilla extract, gravies, ice cream, ice cream cones, gelatin mixes, high fructose corn syrup, frozen flavored yogurt, ice milk, modified food starch, "blended oils" without specification about their derivations, butterscotch Life Savers and chewing gum.

It is even an ingredient in aspirin, cough syrup and lozenges, the gum on envelopes, stamps, stickers and tapes, talcum powders, toothpastes, vitamin coatings, plastic food wrappers (inner surfaces may be coated with cornstarch), and paper cups.

Although the frequency of food allergy to wheat and corn is approximately the same, say experts, commercial corn products cause more reactions. Why? Because corn is often soaked in sulfur dioxide for days in order to separate the kernel into different parts.

In fact, the very processing of corn begins with immersion of the whole kernel in a sulfur dioxide solution. This practice prevents fermentation of the corn while it is being processed. But it also contaminates all manufactured corn products with sulfur, which is itself a major allergen. The basic sources of corn are cornmeal, cornstarch, corn flour, corn syrup, corn sugar, and corn oil. So read labels!

Alternatives? See the next chapter.

Chocolate

CAN CHOCOLATE TURN YOU INTO A CRIMINAL? SOME EXPERTS SAY SO, runs a headline in the *Wall Street Journal.* Staff reporter Timothy D. Schellhardt quotes K. E. Moyer, a psychology professor at Carnegie-Mellon University: "While a person who is allergic to pollen may have a stuffy nose, a person allergic to chocolate . . . may pass out bloody noses."

Why? Because the cocoa bean is a major allergen and with its large amount of sensitizing, nerve-jangling sugar and blood-sugar lowering caffeine,° it is one of our top food allergens, capable of causing serious behavior problems.

According to Dr. William H. Philpott, a psychiatrist and specialist in cerebral allergies, there is a direct correlation between foods such as chocolate, and crime, at least when the eater is biochemically chocolate intolerant: "Food allergies directly affect the body's nervous system by causing a noninflammatory swelling of the brain, which can trigger aggression."

° Candy bars and cocoa products contain only 6 to 30 milligrams of caffeine in commonly consumed portions, but one cup of cocoa may contain up to 270 milligrams of the caffeine-related stimulant theobromine.

In Manhasset, New York, Dr. Jose Yaryura-Tobias, psychiatrist and research director at the North Nassau Mental Health Center, treats patients, including lawbreakers whose violent behavior is often food based. One patient, a man arrested for assaulting and injuring his wife, admitted during examination to cravings for chocolate, cola drinks and coffee, all of which made him feel calmer for a few hours after use. Dr. Yaryura-Tobias placed the man on a diet low in carbohydrates and high in proteins and vitamin B_6. "He improved within eight weeks," the doctor says.

"The top allergy culprit in kids [besides milk]," says Dr. William C. Deamer of the University of California School of Medicine at San Francisco, "is chocolate. Together, they are to blame for two-thirds of all allergic food reactions in children. Other food items that should be checked out if a child shows allergy symptoms are: cola, citrus fruits and juices, eggs, tomatoes, legumes, wheat, apples, cinnamon, rice, and food coloring."

Antisocial behavior is only one of the serious effects food allergies produce. Of the 5.5 million children who are bed wetters, research indicates chocolate is second only to milk when the cause is a food allergen.

Chocolate causes constipation, rectal itch, and has been indicted as a cause of migraines because it is high in amines (other sources of amines include coffee, tea, alcohol, citrus fruit, and cheese). "An excess of amines produces a lowering of blood pressure, a pooling of blood in capillary beds, and a resultant increase in intracranial pressure which can cause severe headaches," says the National Migraine Foundation. Sensitivity to chocolate usually calls for elimination of cola and cocoa products as well as chocolate.

Easy to decide to do. Hard to do, if you are a chocoholic. We spend $3.4 billion a year on chocolate and cocoa, and we eat nine to fourteen pounds per capita, relishing every bite because chocolate is habituating, as Natalie Golos points out in *Coping with Your Allergies.*

A case in point? "Chuck was a classic case of food addiction," says Golos. He would go to a neighborhood store and buy several kinds of chocolate cookies and chocolate candy and gobble them all down in the space of an hour. He would be sick the next day, but as soon as he had money he would do the same thing. Some days Chuck would come home from school and become hysterical, screaming for something to eat. It was found that Chuck's craving for chocolate was an addiction. When he couldn't have chocolate, he suffered withdrawal symptoms, much in the manner of a drug addict withdrawing from drugs."

Another reason chocolate and cocoa are such highly allergenic substances is that they are not as simple as they seem. According to the FDA, chocolate is a so-called Standards of Identity food, meaning that chocolate isn't *all* you get in a chocolate bar. Rather than require a full listing of mandatory ingredients on the label (which consumers are presumed to know), the FDA merely records them in the Code of Federal Regulations (which consumers are also presumed to know about).

Chocolate and cocoa are not interchangeable but you can't have one without the other. Here's how we get from cocoa bean to chocolate bar: After the bean is roasted and the fibrous shell removed, it is ground as finely as possible, producing bitter chocolate or "chocolate liquor," as it is called. This is common baking chocolate, as sugar and flavorings haven't been added. Chocolate liquor is very high in fat, and the fat, or cocoa butter, can be easily removed by pressing, or extracting with a solvent.

If enough fat is removed so that what is left is a powder instead of a paste, you have cocoa powder which may contain anywhere from 23 percent fat to as little as 10 percent. The flavor and quality of the cocoa as well as the price is generally related to its content: The more cocoa butter, the higher the price.

The three main substances derived from the cocoa bean are chocolate liquor, cocoa, and cocoa butter used to make fudge, chocolate coatings, and chocolate bars. Sugar, milk, lecithin, and flavor are used in processing milk chocolate, and sweet or semisweet chocolate results if milk is *not* used. Cocoa butter is a nongreasy fat that is hard at temperatures just below body temperature, and melts quickly and pleasantly in the mouth. Because of this, it is widely used in foods, cosmetics, and pharmaceuticals. Cocoa's flavor can be upgraded and darkened by treating it with an alkali such as potassium carbonate, a process called "dutching." Dutched cocoa does not refer to imported cocoa, but to cocoa chemically treated. The process is considered harmless by the FDA.

Chocolate has a few features in its favor. Two ounces of milk chocolate supply 4.3 grams of protein (incomplete), 32 grams of get-you-going carbohydrate, 127 milligrams of calcium, 129 milligrams of phosphorus, 215 milligrams of potassium, and 151 units of Vitamin A.

But two ounces also supply cholesterol, 11 grams of unhealthy saturated fat, and almost 300 calories, along with small amounts of caffeine, traces of theophylline, and large amounts of theobromine. These last three substances are central nervous system stimulants called methylxanthines found in tea and coffee as well.

Chocolate is present in chocolate candy, baking chocolate, chocolate drink mixes, and cocoa. Nothing but improved health and a reduction in allergic sensitivity can come from eliminating chocolate from your dessert life. If you need a crutch and miss the taste, carob can help. It's a low-calorie chocolate taste-alike, highly nutritious, caffeine- and sugar-free, and even available in supermarkets.

Botanically, chocolate belongs to the *Sterculia* or *Theobroma* family which also includes cocoa, the kola nut, and gum karaya.

See the alternatives to chocolate in chapter II.

Soybeans

Too much of a good thing can be bad. In fact, in 95 percent of all food allergy cases, reactions are caused by eating too much of a single specific food. This certainly puts soybeans on the spot since they appear on everybody's dessert menu—if not by choice, by accident.

Soybeans are one of the five foods (the other four are cow's milk, peanuts, nuts, and eggs) cited as "important causes of allergic symptoms" in a recent study of one hundred infants and children. What sort of symptoms are soybeans responsible for? Those that are referred to as *"allergic mediated reactions,"* in which symptoms appear a few minutes to a few hours after ingestion of the food and are manifested by hives, rashes, asthma, diarrhea, and vomiting or abdominal pain, to name but a few.

And according to Dr. Hugh Sampson, a pediatric allergist at Duke University in Durham, North Carolina, 50 percent of children who have eczema, a disfiguring skin ailment are allergic to one of the five foods including soybeans.

The *good* news is that, according to the Allergy and Asthma Foundation of America, most children outgrow this allergy. "But while they remain sensitive, soybeans should be avoided in any form," suggests Dr. Sampson.

Soybeans are considered by many authorities to be the biggest offender among the vegetable allergens. In adults, since the digestive system is matured and less vulnerable, the target may be the skeletal system. Rheumatoid arthritis is considered to be an *autoimmune disease,* meaning a reaction occurs whereby you become allergic to your own body substances. An allergic response to a frequently eaten substance such as soybean may induce joint pain and even swelling.

Or sometimes the skin is affected. In angioedema, the tongue or throat area may be swollen, causing obstruction of the airways, or small hemorrhages can occur in the skin causing what looks like tiny bruises, called purpura. This is a manifestation of an allergic disturbance of the normal blood-clotting mechanisms and it is one possible reaction if you eat soybean-containing foods and have a pronounced sensitivity to them.

Two factors that can make your soybean-related suffering insufferable are stress and alcohol. An allergic person is 50 percent more likely than someone non-allergic to react when he or she is under pressure, and alcohol, says Dr. Lawrence Lamb, "dilates the small blood vessels, allowing more of the offending food protein to be picked up."

Losing soybeans as a dessert ingredient is a loss but not a *great* loss. One-half a cup of soybeans gives you 118 calories, 9.8 grams of protein (complete), 5.1 grams of fat, 10.1 grams of carbohydrate, 60 milligrams of calcium, 191 milligrams of phosphorus, 2.5 milligrams of iron, 660 units of vitamin A, 13 milligrams of B_2, and 1.2 milligrams of niacin.

Soybeans contain no cholesterol and are rich in linoleic acid, an unsaturated fatty acid needed for growth and for the health of the hair, skin, and glands. But soybean protein is very low in vitamin C, and other nutritious bean flours are available if you can't have wheat as well (see the Wheat section earlier in this chapter).

But sidestepping this good-but-sometimes-offending food is easier said than done.

Sources of soybeans? You'd be amazed. They're found in soy flour, soy granules, soy grits, soy lecithin° (powdered, liquid, and granules), soy milk, soy nuts, soy oil, soy sauce or shoyu sauce, miso, and tofu. Not to mention store-bought breads, baby formulas, candy, cereals, ice creams and ice cream cones, lunch meats, margarine, puddings, snack foods including corn and potato chips, synthetic spices, coffee substitutes and drink mixes, and virtually every type of baked good from coffee cake to waffles!

Soy lecithin is even used as a stabilizer in leaded gasoline, and if you tend to have "contact allergies" (skin reactions from coming in contact with an allergen), watch out.

According to Texas researcher Dorothy W. Brown, the Ford Motor Company has used soybean to make plastic window frames, steering wheels, gear shift knobs, distributors and

---

° Soybeans are a common source of lecithin, but not all lecithin is derived from soybeans. Widely used by the food industry as an emulsifying agent, the exact source is rarely noted on labels. Manufacturers are not obligated to list the source of the lecithin used in their products, and the source of the lecithin can change without notice.

other parts, as well as an upholstery fabric. Rubber substitutes and lecithin in leaded gasoline are made from soybeans. Some cosmetics contain soybean oil, and it is found in many plastic products such as telephones, toys, clothing.

Soybeans (including lecithin and tofu) belong to the legume family. For alternatives to soybeans see the next chapter.

Eggs

According to a national food survey, 11 percent of us don't eat eggs. Since up to 93 percent of us with food allergies are allergic to them, that's just as well. Eggs were the first common food linked specifically to allergy. A New York pediatrician first diagnosed the allergy in a child in 1912.

An allergy to eggs shouldn't be treated lightly. According to the allergist Claude A. Frazier from Asheville, North Carolina, "Even the odors of some foods—eggs . . . for example— can affect those who are allergic to them . . . some individuals are so hypersensitive that they suffer allergy symptoms if they even touch such foods or are kissed by someone who has just eaten them. This is especially true of those sensitive to eggs."

Consider the case of the physician generally credited with discovery of the principle of "hidden" or "masked" food allergy, Dr. Herbert J. Rinkel:

"Although he [Rinkel] consulted several different physicians, the cause of his profuse rhinorrhea [running nose] was not determined . . . but . . . several years later, he happened to avoid eggs along with several other foods, while testing the assumption that foods might be involved. After eliminating eggs in all forms from his diet for about five days, he ate a piece of angel food cake at a birthday party. Within a few minutes he lapsed into a state of profound physical collapse.

Pulse, blood pressure, respiratory rate, neurological and other finds were within normal limits; unconsciousness was his only symptom.

"To test his suspicion that eggs were the cause, Rinkel began eating eggs again. He then omitted eggs again for five days, repeated the egg ingestion, and experienced another bout of unconsciousness. . . ."

He may have been the first to react this way but he won't be the last.

Eggs, a food which many of us eat daily, can cause serious illness. According to Kate Ludeman, Ph.D., and Louise Henderson, authors of *The Do It Yourself Allergy Analysis Handbook*:

"Cumulative allergic reactions to foods may develop slowly over a period of time. If you are allergic to a food and eat it two or three times a week, there is *never* a time when your body is free of that food, thus it accumulates to a level that exceeds your tolerance. This results in a series of continuing allergic reactions in which one reaction begins before the previous reaction subsides. This often causes a serious chronic illness. Although you may be sick most of the time, you may never realize that your chronic illness is caused by cumulative food allergy."

Eggs are not inherently bad. They are a nutritional bargain if you can handle them. The only protein considered by nutrition experts to be better than eggs is mother's milk. Eggs supply first-class complete protein, a fair amount of vitamin A, all the B vitamins, as well as vitamin E, iron, and many other minerals and trace minerals, and there are only 80 calories in an egg, a bonus for weight watchers.

What else? Eggs contain more of the two amino acids (links of protein), methionine and cysteine, which contain the trace mineral sulfur, than any other food except Brazil nuts. Sulfur, long used to heal psoriasis, is essential for healthy skin, hair, nails and joints. It also is a component of insulin, the deficient hormone in diabetics.

Eggs are also considered to be "food relaxants" because they are rich in choline, an amino acid derivative important to the proper functioning of the parasympathetic nervous system that controls glandular activity, blood flow, and sleep.

But if it's got to be sunnyside down for you, it's gotta be. If you love your desserts, it won't be easy to eliminate eggs or to drastically reduce their use, but it *is* possible. The problem is that eggs are everywhere. Even when you don't deliberately eat them you get them. Who would consider Quaker's 100% Natural Cereal or A&W Root Beer as egg allergen sources? But they are. Eggs, along with wheat, milk, soybeans, cane sugar, and yeast, are a major hidden food offender. For example, egg whites are used often as a glaze on bakery goods and candies and need not be mentioned on the label. Egg white is also used to produce the foam in soft drinks and to clarify wines, coffee, and consommés, and foods are often dipped in eggs even though eggs are not part of the main ingredient.

If you're avoiding eggs, some of the sweet stuff to look out for include *most* candy bars and novelties as well as chocolate creams, marshmallows, custards, eggnog, frozen custard, ice cream and sherbets, blancmange, cream pies, frostings, macaroons, meringes, pastries, puddings, "whips," French toast and blintzes.

So scrutinize ingredients panels. Prepackaged desserts, especially baked foods, contain eggs in some form. When eating out or at home, skip foods cooked in batters, breadings, or pastries, since eggs are a common binder. Check the recipes on egg-free packaged mixes that require you to add eggs, and watch out for these terms on labels: DRIED EGGS, EGG ALBUMIN (OVALBUMIN), EGG WHITE SOLIDS, EGG WHITES, EGG YOLK SOLIDS, POWDERED EGGS, and WHOLE EGGS.

Eggs belong to the pheasant food family, which also includes chicken, peafowl, quail, and, of course, pheasant.

For some sound alternatives to eggs see the following chapter.

Nuts

Some experts estimate that 100 percent of all human illness involves food intolerance. And one of the foods we especially don't tolerate is nuts, either alone or as "hidden" offenders in hundreds of dessert and snack-type foods.

The clinical allergist, J. C. Breneman, M.D., reports a positive response in 14.5 percent of patients tested for nut sensitivity, putting nuts in the big leagues with other offenders such as beans and corn.

Nuts can present you with any one of those persistent but not life-threatening ailments that resist traditional therapy— which is just another way of saying food allergy. Pistachio addiction could make you a migraine cripple, walnuts could give you insomnia, or maybe it's pecans that make you puff up like a blowfish. "Edema is one of the most common symptoms of allergy," notes specialist Dr. Jonathan V. Wright.

And Dr. Theron G. Randolph, writing about what he terms "minus three" and "minus four" allergic reactions, includes walnuts as causes of depression, headaches, and fatigue.

And if you can't stop after one peanut or cashew, you're not alone. "Once I start eating," said one of Dr. Randolph's patients, whose favorite food was peanut butter*—the one item she could not do without—"I feel as if I cannot stop."

Holiday goodies loaded with lots of nuts, which in turn are loaded with lots of an amino acid known as arginine, are even a cause of herpes sores, says Dr. Richard J. Griffith, a professor of medicine at Indiana University School of Medicine in Indianapolis.

Nuts are nutritious if you can tolerate them. Besides potassium and magnesium, minerals often deficient in the diets of people under allergic stress, they provide rich supplies of linoleic acid, an unsaturated fat necessary for energy, growth, and the production of beneficial intestinal bacteria that produces B vitamins. Linoleic acid also helps prevent water retention and slows down the conversion of sugars into fat in the body, as well as satisfying hunger. Thirty to forty walnuts could provide your Recommended Daily Allowance (RDA) for protein if taken with a little milk or cheese.

What can you do if you are a nut-sensitive nut-nut? Avoid the ones that offend, explore the ones that are left, or switch

---

* Actually, the peanut is a legume. But it is commonly eaten as a nut food and used as a dessert ingredient.

to roasted beans for a snack. Use sprouts, granola, or cereal brands in their place. It may make matters better to take a little antihistamine if your allergy is mild and when you munch, munch some of the more exotic nuts such as macadamia, pine nuts, Indian (betel) nuts, or litchis.

On the other hand, it will definitely make matters worse if you binge on the nut you're sensitive to during hay fever season. Two allergic stresses can have the biochemical impact of ten then.

What else should you pass up besides peanut brittle and trail mix? Licorice and maybe even carob. Both are in the same botanical family along with soybeans.

The nut family is actually several families. The walnut family includes butternuts, hickory nuts, pecans, and walnuts. Each nut in the following list is a separate food family: Brazil nut, chestnut, filbert (hazelnut), litchi nut, macadamia nut, pine nut. Cashews belong to the family that includes pistachios and the tropical fruit mango; almonds are members of the plum family; peanuts belong to the legumes (see Soybeans).

For alternatives to nuts, see the next chapter.

Citrus

Getting juiced? If it's on orange juice, maybe it's not such a good idea.

Of the Americans questioned in a recent survey, 63 percent said they never or almost never touched the stuff.

The orange may not be a "lemon" nutritionally, but allergically it's got a lot to answer for.

If there are any forbidden fruits in your diet, citrus in general and oranges in particular are probably it.

Oranges are a more potent source of allergic reactions than

corn, beans, nuts, peanuts, or tomatoes. What kind of reactions? You name it. Skin rashes are common. So are headaches which, according to Dr. Seymour Diamond, president of the National Migraine Foundation, occur because oranges produce excess levels of a body chemical called amines in some sensitive individuals (chocolate, tea, and coffee are also high in amines).

Citrus can even induce antisocial behavior. Alexander G. Schauss, director of the American Institute for Biosocial Research in Tacoma, Washington, cites the case of a child who, only eight minutes after eating two slices of citric fruit, became hyperactive. In twenty minutes the boy was manic depressive. The boy, Schauss says, was simply allergic to oranges.

Another case of citrus mischief is cited by Dr. Theron G. Randolph in his book, *Human Ecology and Susceptibility to the Chemical Environment:*

"One of the first foods Ralph was tested on was orange juice, because of his addictive-like craving for it. At first he seemed normal, but within about two hours he was flushed in the face, had started to pack his bags, and insulted his mother. . . . Ralph struck his mother twice before his father and I arrived on the scene simultaneously. The room was completely disheveled. When I suggested that the oranges were the cause of this reaction, he started screaming and tore his symptom chart to shreds. . . ."

Technically speaking, the orange is a berry with a reddish-yellow leathery, aromatic rind grown domestically in California and Florida. California types are more orange in color, thicker skinned, and less juicy than the Florida types. (The best Florida varieties, say experts, are the Parson Brown, the Pineapple orange, and the Temple orange.) Most California oranges are of the navel variety, famous for their seedlessness.

Orange juice contains magnesium, sulfur, and a very high amount of calcium and phosphorus. Eight ounces supplies 625 units of vitamin A; plus vitamin B_1, vitamin B_2, and about 120 milligrams of vitamin C, along with 2 grams of protein. Orange juice assists in bone formation, supplies lots of real fruit sugar, and is reputedly a good body cleanser.

But oranges aren't good for you if they make you feel bad. And passing them up, along with the rest of the citrus family, isn't easy. Oranges are omnipresent in our diet. Industry finds a use for every part of the orange. Margarine and other cooking fats are derived from the seeds; a dye is derived from the skin to fix the colors in some synthetic fabrics; the peel is used in paint; pectin from the pulp is used as a jelling agent in preserves, even in the treatment of wounds. Finally, the residue is fed to cattle, and from the water in which the peel is washed comes tons of molasses. Oranges are said to aid in the digestion of milk.

One thing industry has *little* use for is nature, which didn't intend our most celebrated citrus to be the color orange. Most oranges are ripe when bright green. And did you know all oranges are tree ripened? They do not ripen after being picked, like some fruit. But colder temperatures *can* cause an orange to turn from green to orange, so green and yellowish-green oranges are often placed in a "degreening" room where ethylene, a gas to which many allergy victims are sensitive, is used to decompose the chlorophyll (green), giving the fruit an orange pigment. That's not all. Oranges are scrubbed, moisture is removed to lengthen shelf life and they are often dyed and waxed.

Eating or cooking the peels of commercial oranges can be especially hazardous if you are allergic. DBCP, a chemical used to produce the same result as the propionate bakeries use to keep breads fresh, is routinely applied to oranges. So is sodium o-phenol, which retards spoilage and shrinkage and provides fresher-appearing, longer-lasting oranges. It is foamed onto the surface of the fruit, rinsed off with fresh water, usually leaving a residue.

If you're leaving oranges *out* of your diet, you can get vitamin C into it by taking an ascorbic acid supplement. As healthy as citrus fruits are, they haven't got it all. Buffered-C or calcium ascorbate are the types best tolerated by allergy sufferers. There are also plenty of other fruits that can take the place of citrus—the pineapple, for instance.

It is with good reason that the pineapple is known as a tropical wonder fruit. Raw pineapple contains bromelain, a protein-dissolving enzyme that has the ability to break up congestion in the walls of blood vessels. This enzyme can restore permeability and drain toxic wastes that otherwise impair circulation and cause edema.

And if your orange juice allergies make you tense, the juice of a fruit you *can* tolerate can practically be magic. Juice has what are called "psychotropic" qualities, meaning they are capable of altering certain components of the brain, providing relief from mild tension. Juice has a soothing effect on the hypothalamus (emotional center of the brain), creating an overall feeling of relaxation. Blueberries, pineapple, melons, strawberries, and papaya all supply more than 50 milligrams of vitamin C per cup along with their luscious flavors. And all can be used as orange juice alternatives.

What else contains vitamin C besides citrus fruits? Vegetables, berries and herbs. Try black currants, cabbage, chiles, dock, nasturtium flowers, peppers, and herbs such as strawberry leaves, violet leaves, and rosehips.

The citrus family includes citron, angostura, grapefruit, limes, lemons, oranges, tangerines, even kumquats and mandarin oranges. If you are orange sensitive you may also be troubled by citric acid in processed foods. Read labels before you buy. Citrus alternatives? See the next chapter.

Baking Yeast and Food Yeast

Yeast. It gets you up. It gets you down.

And you get it everywhere. Yeast occurs in the form of bakers' yeast cakes, baking granules, food supplements such as

brewers' and nutritional yeast, in natural B-vitamin supplements, in beer and wine and vinegar, in leavened bread, even
sourdough breads (sourdough starters are yeasts, too), most
cheeses, and any foods based on mold or fermentation (i.e.,
sauerkraut). Yeast is also found in not-so-fresh fruit. A moldy
orange, in other words, is as much a source of yeast as a slice
of homemade bread. Research indicates that dried fruits are
also frequently contaminated with yeast spores.

If yeast-raised bread and mold-containing cheese is your
daily bread and butter, you could be unknowingly making
yourself seriously ill with daily overdoses of the famous fungus
among us. (And don't forget to add mushrooms either—they're
close relatives of yeast.)

A few of the dozens of dessert-type store-bought products
containing this allergen include pastries, some cereals (Corn
Chex and Instant Quaker Oatmeal are two), some candies and
most snack foods, coffee lighteners, and root beers containing
real root beer extract. Some allergists caution that malted
foods contain bakers' yeast as well.

Yeast allergy may not be our number one enemy allergy,
but it certainly makes the top ten, causing such well-
documented symptoms in the sensitive as fluid retention (you
may not be fat, you may just have a yeast allergy); uncon-
trollable binge eating; hyperactivity, and such minor an-
noyances as eye blinking, ringing ears (tinnitus), facial tics,
allergic "shiners" (bags under the eyes, which is a frequent
sign of intolerance to a food or chemicals).

Yeast foods are good foods. That's why they're so widely
used and so hard to avoid. But they can be bad foods, too.

On the plus side, *Saccharomyces cerevisiae*, commonly referred to as "brewers' yeast" (which is considered nutritionally superior to the many other types of yeast), is one of
the best natural sources of the entire B-vitamin complex, and
a superior source of concentrated protein, including *all* the
essential amino acids. Additionally, it is rich in nucleic acid, a
basic element in cell development believed to retard the aging
process and is the best nutritional source of chromium, which

occurs as an organic compound known as GTF (Glucose Tolerance Factor), essential for the production of functionally effective insulin.

Yeast also provides plenty of the cancer-fighting, stress-reducing antioxidant trace mineral selenium, says biochemist Carl C. Pfeiffer.

Baking yeast, which is alive food unlike nutritional yeast, also adds B vitamins, protein, and minerals to any diet. So do cheeses and cheese by-products such as whey and buttermilk, which are also yeast sources. But on the minus side, yeast is a very concentrated protein that is often hard to digest, and unless a nutritional yeast is fortified, it can provide you with too much phosphorus and too little calcium—a dangerous situation that can contribute to osteoporosis. But the biggest minus of all is yeast's role as an allergen.

Chiropractor Gerald Stavish, founder of the Ecology Center, describes allergic reactions as "symptoms of the inefficiency of body machinery in its adaption to environmental situations." The yeast you're getting in your daily dessert—whether it's a piece of cake or a glass of sweet wine—can make a heavy contribution to such inefficiency.

And according to allergist Dr. William H. Philpott, alcoholic addiction results from a cerebral allergy to the fermentable substances on which the yeast-food-alcohol mixture is based. An alcoholic is really someone suffering from allergic addiction to the corn, rye, wheat, brewers' yeast, malt, or other ingredients that ferment into the alcoholic beverage.

Another problem is that yeast supplements are often grown on sugar beet molasses. If you are sugar sensitive, such a yeast is double trouble. And, according to Dr. Marshall Mandell, the country's foremost authority on mold allergy, yeast can bring on "brain fag" in the form of chronic fatigue, depression, and mental confusion along with such old standby symptoms as stuffy sinuses, asthma, and a runny nose.

Avoid all baked goods made with yeast. A leavening provided by baking soda or baking powder is safe. Read labels and stay away from highly processed foods as much as possible, as well as fresh foods that are going bad. They are certain to be a source of mold and thus yeast.

All yeast belongs to the fungi family, which includes brewers' yeast, all types of nutritional yeast, mold foods such as cheeses, morels, mushrooms, truffles, malt, and citric acid.

See the following chapter for some alternatives to yeast.

Food Additives

"Ninety-four percent of the hyperactive kids I've seen are allergic to food colors of some sort," says one pediatrician specializing in allergy control. "With an elimination diet, I've found there's a five- or six-to-one chance the behavior can be controlled without drugs."

Allergic hyperactivity afflicts over 5 million children and it's even a problem for some adults. (For more details write to the Feingold Association of the United States, Drawer A-G, Holtsville, NY 11742.)

Food colors° are widely used in sweet foods. Maraschino cherries are produced by packing red cherries in sulfur dioxide brine, bleaching out the color, and removing natural juices and sugars. The resulting pale yellow cherry is then soaked with red dye, sugar, and the artificial flour benzaldehyde. About 11,308 pounds of artificial red dye alone are used to color maraschino cherries each year. In fact, 90 percent of the 1,000 dyes in use in food today are synthetic.

° Note: The United States government certifies "pure" but this means only that they are coal tar–derived colors meeting certain specifications, not that they are healthy, safe, or that people do not react adversely. "Government certification does not consider their biologic activity as allergic excitants," says Dr. Marshall Mandell, "and artificial colors and flavors cause more than hyperactivity. Any food color can produce different symptoms in different people, including adults."

And every year turns up something new. In December 1980, the National Cancer Institute announced it had found that a synthetic additive used as an imitation grape or cherry flavor since 1940 caused cancer of the liver, pancreas, and kidney in animals. Five hundred pounds of this chemical and 75,000 pounds of other synthetic grape flavors plus 250,000 pounds of other synthetic cherry flavors are used every year in food.

Or consider FD&C yellow no. 5. *The New England Journal of Medicine* reports that between 50,000 and 100,000 Americans are allergic to this food color. Ingestion of the foods containing this dye can cause bronchial asthma, inflammation of the mucous membranes in the nose, hives, severe itching of the skin, and a buildup of fluid in body tissues. A few common foods and drinks containing FD&C yellow no. 5 are: Tang, Awake, and Daybreak orange drinks; some Jell-O instant pudding and pie fillings; certain flavors of Jell-O and Royal gelatins; lime-flavored Gatorade; Jewel imitation lemonade mix, various cake mixes and cake icings. Also McCormick imitation butter flavoring, imitation banana extract, and imitation pineapple extract; Brach's lemon drops, butterscotch, and candy corn; and Planters Cheez Curls and Cheez Balls.

Food coloring is found in butter, certain fruits (e.g., oranges), fruit juices, margarine, soft drinks, baked goods, cherries, ice creams, cake mixes, and candies. And if your sweet tooth extends to toothpastes and mouthwashes, these are usually artificially colored and flavored, too.

Besides food colors, there are flavoring agents such as vanillin, benzaldehyde, eucalyptol, and MSG routinely used in fruit-flavored drinks, gelatins, candies, sodas, and frozen desserts.

According to British dermatologist Dr. Lennart Juhlin, one-third of all patients tested show one or more positive reactions to food additives such as BHT, BHA, sorbic acid, benzoates, and annato, all of which are used in commercial desserts, with hives (or urticaria) the most common symptom.

And unfortunately, where you find phony food dyes, you usually find food coloring.

Here are the ingredients in a best-selling pudding dessert sold by one of America's largest manufacturers of ready-to-eat desserts: skim milk (vitamin A added), sugar, water, nonfat dry milk, hydrogenated coconut and palm kernel oils, corn syrup, modified tapioca starch, dextrin (from tapioca), sodium caseinate (a protein), salt, dextrose (corn sugar), sodium stearol lactylate (emulsifier for uniform dispersion of oils), artificial flavor, polysorbate 60 (emulsifier), microcrystalline cellulose (for smooth texture), sorbitan monostearate (emulsifier), xanthan gum, carrageenin, cellulose gum and guar gum (thickeners), and artificial color. Plus either caramel color or yellow no. 5. There is no banana in the banana flavor and no real vanilla in the vanilla version.

What kind of symptoms can chemicals cause besides too much get up and go? Or too little? (There is an allergic response called *hypo*activity, too, characterized by very *slow* motion activity.)

Dr. Mandell discusses the case history of one patient in *Dr. Mandell's Five-Day Allergy Relief System:*

"Even when some acceptable foods were given to David in their commercial form, however, they caused grimaces . . . eye circles, and gassiness. . . . The boy became progressively more grouchy and twitchy after the second feeding of 'normal' food, and this increased with each subsequent feeding. The avoidance of such foods paved the way for David's recovery. . . . He was one of those hyperactive children whose problem was actually caused by a highly individualized reaction to food and chemical environment. . . . One person will get a headache; another will have asthma. Someone else may have abdominal discomfort or joint pains or itching or become restless or depressed. One of my pediatric patients had a bladder reaction with painful urination. . . ."

Unfortunately, additive rich desserts are the rule rather than the exception. What to do?

Look for the products with the fewest ingredients, or do without it. Raw fruits are still the best nutritional bet when the pantry's bare. And remember, nobody will arrest you for having a salad instead of a cookie for dessert, either.

Best of all, make it yourself. You save yourself and your children from stress, disease, excess calories, and a guilty conscience. Natural alternatives to unnatural food colors and flavors appear throughout this book.

Spices

Among the "unsuspected, uncommon forms of allergy," cited by allergist Doris J. Rapp, author of *Allergies and the Hyperactive Child*, are excessive throat mucus, excessive perspiration, clucking throat sounds, and a mottled tongue.

And if you've already written off such dessert ingredient offenders as chocolate, sugar, milk, eggs, and corn, consider spices.

Although they are responsible for only a third of the reactions caused by oranges, soybeans, and nuts, spices cause more flare-ups than a grain like rye. And the reason they make the lists is, of course, because we tend to use the same spices— nutmeg, cinnamon, and ginger, for example—over and over. And for that 75 percent of the population prone to develop sensitivities, spice abuse leads to food allergy.

According to Dr. S. Allan Bock, pediatric allergist at the National Jewish Hospital–National Asthma Center in Denver, spices rank tenth just after peas and beans on the "foods most commonly incriminated in food allergies."

Why? Because the trouble with spice allergy detection and control is that next to additives and sugar, there's nothing manufacturers love more, or use more, or hide more. We import over 400 million pounds of spice a year. U.S. consumption of spices continues to increase faster than the growth rate of the population, with sales estimated at over $870 million.

And they go into everything from cake mix to caramels—

usually without label declaration. If you love desserts, you're probably getting enough of the commoner spices to set you up for symptoms without realizing it. Why? Because eating a potential food offender two or three times a week means your body is never free of that food. And when it reaches a level you can no longer tolerate, your reaction may cause and even perpetuate a serious illness.

If you are spice sensitive, on the other hand, maybe you're better off. All the returns aren't in, but according to studies by a scientist from the University of Kentucky presented to the American Chemical Society, a wide variety of flavorings, including cinnamon, vanilla, and anise, contain chemicals that may induce tumors. Malignant tumors, sometimes in several organs, were observed in mice treated with spices.

Also, on the positive side, spices are *not* an essential. They're a nice but optional part of your dessert diet. And if cinnamon is out, that doesn't exclude cardamom or chamomile, which taste just as nice and are in no way botanically related.

If you suspect sensitivity, the best thing is to skip the spice, reduce the amount you use, or switch to something else. (See following chapter.)

Botanically, ginger belongs to the ginger family, which also includes cardamom and turmeric. Vanilla comes from vanilla beans, which belong to the orchid family. Cinnamon belongs to the laurel family, which also includes avocado and sassafras. Mint belongs to the mint family, which includes lavender, thyme, and horehound among others. Clove and allspice belong to the myrtle family along with paprika. Nutmeg and mace are the only members of the nutmeg family.

II.   The Top Alternatives
to Dessert Allergens

NOTE: The numbers below are your guide to the where-abouts of the ingredients discussed in this chapter.

1.   Most supermarkets.
2.   Health food stores, herb and spice suppliers, specialty food shops.
3.   Mail order. See sources in Appendix B.

Alternatives to Sugar

About the Sweeteners

Raw honey. Look for the words RAW or UNPASTEURIZED or UNFILTERED on the label. Also look for a source such as clover, tupelo, buckwheat, or the like. Darker honey is healthier, so is

honey in the comb, most crystallized honey, and honey produced locally.

Barley malt and blackstrap molasses. Blackstrap molasses or
barley malt are concentrated sweeteners which, unlike refined
sugar products, are rich in nutrients. Malt, which is made by
slowly cooking sprouted barley, contains B-complex vitamins,
the amino acid lysine, and many essential minerals. Blackstrap
molasses, which is the residue of the sugarcane after the sugar
is extracted, contains more iron per unit of weight than eggs,
more calcium than milk, more potassium than any other food,
and is rich in several other minerals and vitamins. But it is
more bitter than sweet. Combine with honey or fruit juice to
use as a sweetener.

Date sugar. Not a real "sugar" at all, just dried dates that
have been dehydrated and pulverized into granular form. Like
maple syrup, it's very tasty, very nutritious, but not as sweet
as refined sugar and has poor dissolving properties. Also costly
at three dollars to four dollars for twelve ounces and you don't
save on calories. But dates are rich in all the important minerals and trace minerals plus a few vitamins. And as a sugar
replacement it is perfect for sweetening cereal, yogurt, ice
cream, and fruit salad.

Maple sugar and maple syrup granules. If there's such a
thing as a newfangled, old-fashioned substitute, this is it. Maple syrup in a crystalline form is fairly new. It isn't any lower
in calories than regular sugar but it does contain more nutrients—especially B vitamins and the energizing mineral
potassium—than any other sweetener. It also has as much calcium as milk and only one-tenth the sodium of honey. It tastes
better than sucrose even if it has poor dissolving properties.
Expensive but worth it. So is real maple syrup.

Rice syrup and carob syrup. These are expensive but worth
the price if you are sensitive to honey, maple syrup, and fruits.
Both supply considerable amounts of B-vitamin complex and
moderate amounts of minerals.

If you're allergic to sugar . . .

Sources

1.   Replace granulated sugar with any natural dry

sugar such as date sugar (made from dates), maple
syrup granules, barley malt granules or powder, or any
homemade dry sugar (see chapter V, Recipes,
Homemade Sugars, Sweeteners, and Syrups).
Remember, these sugars are only half as sweet as
refined sugar so you usually have to use twice as much.
If you use more, increase the liquid in your recipe,
too, by at least ¼ cup or as needed.   2, 3
2.   Replace granulated sugar with any natural liquid
sweetener—except honey—in the same amount.
Examples: maple syrup, barley malt, syrup, carob
syrup, fig syrup, sorghum, unsulfured molasses, rice
syrup. Honey is sweeter than dry refined sugar. Use
less of any type liquid sweetener.° Blackstrap molasses
is highly nutritious but slightly bitter.   2, 3
3.   A cup of any dry natural sugar combined with any
natural liquid sweetener. To replace a cup of
granulated sugar try ½ cup honey plus ¼ cup date
sugar, for example.   2, 3
4.   Carob powder (see Alternatives to Chocolate)
adds a low level of sweetness and a pseudo-chocolate
flavor to desserts. Whey powder and milk powder also
lend a low-voltage sweetness, but avoid them if you
are milk intolerant.   2, 3
5.   Reduce calories and add vitamins by using 1
tablespoon of sugar-free fruit juice concentrate to
replace 1 tablespoon of an undesirable sweetener such
as corn syrup or even a "good" sugar such as raw
honey.   1, 2
6.   Other ways to make dessert taste sweet without
sugar?   1, 2
   Ripen it. A very ripe banana is lower in starch and
twice as high in natural sugar as a going-on-green
banana. Ditto peaches, pears, and tropical fruits.

° NOTE: To compensate for the added liquid, decrease eggs, milk, or other fluids in
   the recipe or increase amount of dry ingredients such as flour. For example, if
   you use ½ cup honey to replace 1 cup sugar, deduct ¼ cup liquid from recipe.
   Remember, each alternative sweetener has a distinctive flavor of its own. Become acquainted with each one before you make substitutes.

Toast it. Toasted bread is sweeter than plain bread because heat increases dextrins. Ditto toasted dry cereals, rolled oats, and flour.

Apple it up. Apples (especially crab apples) contain plenty of natural pectin so you can use them to thicken jams and bypass sugary commercial pectins. Apples don't dominate the taste of the main fruit. They blend into it. The flavor of apples is compatible with any jam fruit, for example. If you're using apples in a recipe that contains lemon juice, you can use 50 percent less juice because apples are naturally acid.

Sprout it. Sprouting is a sweetening process. Sprouted wheat can be ground to a paste and used to sweeten breads and cakes. Or try sprouted rye, oats, or barley.

Simmer it. Long cooking of any pureed or mashed fruit over surface heat boils off water, thickens fruit pulp, and concentrates natural sweetness: 45 minutes for medium to low-pectin fruits and 30 minutes for high-pectin fruits such as crab apples, red currants, sour plums, and quinces.

Note: 1 tablespoon of sugar alternative replaces 1 tablespoon of refined sugar, except where noted. It also alters flavor.

Alternatives to Regular Dairy Milk and Milk Products

If you're allergic to regular dairy milk:

Sources

1. Try soy milk or goat's milk. Both are available in liquid milk form or evaporated in a can or as a quick powder you can mix yourself.

2, 3

	Sources
2. Use soy powder in place of milk powder (it's available in full-fat and low-fat forms).	2, 3
3. Any fruit juice can be used over hot or cold cereal in place of milk or cream.	1, 2
4. Fruit juice can be substituted for milk in quick baked goods such as muffins, fruit cakes, and pancakes.	1,2
5. Pineapple juice is a good substitute for milk in preparation of oatmeal and other hot cereals.	1, 2
6. Make potato milk: Process 1 peeled potato and ½ cup water in blender, adding more water, if necessary. Sweeten with 1 to 2 teaspoons honey or any homemade sugar (see chapter V, Recipes, Home Sugars, Sweeteners, and Syrups).	1, 2
7. Use 1 cup water, 1 tablespoon lemon juice, and ½ teaspoon baking soda to replace 1 cup milk in breads and other baked goods.	1, 2
8. See recipes for milk substitutes using nuts, vegetables, and sprouts in chapter V, Recipes, Milk and Cream Substitutes.	

If you're allergic to cream. . .

	Sources
1. Use evaporated goat or soy milk.	2, 3
2. Try tofu pureed with water or fruit juice to desired thickness.	2
3. Use powdered soy milk prepared with only half the liquid required (or follow package directions for soy cream).	2, 3
4. Use recipes for homemade creams and whipped topping substitutes in chapter 5, Recipes, Milk and Cream Substitutes and Toppings and Dessert Sauces.	

If you're allergic to butter. . .

	Sources
1 Use 100 percent natural corn oil margarine.	1, 2
2. Use milk-free kosher margarine.	2, 3

3.   Use ⅞ cup vegetable or nut oil in place of 1 cup of
butter.   *1, 2*
4.   Margarines made from soybeans with no
preservatives or artificial colors can be used just as you
would butter or less nutritious supermarket
margarines.   *2, 3*
5.   Replace 1 cup dairy butter in any desserts. Use ½
cup nonmilk margarine and ¼ cup pure vegetable oil.
Can be combined in a "blended butter."   *1, 2*

Note: Animal fats including rendered lamb fat, chicken, goose, and
duck fat are substitutes for butter but not healthy ones—they are
too rich in saturated fats, so avoid them.

Alternatives to Wheat

If you're allergic to wheat. . .°

                                                                          Sources

1.   Substitute one of the following for 1 cup wheat
flour:
   1⅓ cup ground rolled oats, or
   ⅝ cup rice flour plus ⅓ cup rye flour, or
   ½ cup potato flour plus ½ cup rye flour, or
   ½ cup barley flour plus ½ cup potato flour, or
   ¾ cup cornmeal plus ½ cup ground rolled oats, or
   ⅝ cup buckwheat flour † plus ⅓ cup rye flour, or
   1 cup ground oats plus ⅓ cup soy flour †   *2, 3*

° Wheat, rye, barley, and buckwheat are genetically similar. If wheat's an allergen, you may have trouble with the others as well. This is called "cross-
sensitivity," allergists tell us. There is a considerable amount of cross-sensitivity
to the whole cereal grass family, which in addition to these four also includes
corn, millet, oats, rice, and sugarcane.

† These substitutes contain either no or very small amounts of gluten (protein
which occurs in wheat and makes dough elastic and bread light); don't use
bakers' yeast (except with all rye flour), use a yeast substitute instead (see Alternatives to Baking Yeast).

2.   Replace some or all flour in piecrusts and cookies
with ground nuts. The more finely a nut is ground the
more oily it becomes, providing greater binding
property.   1, 2
3.   Wheat germ alternatives include:
   Oven-toasted rolled oats
   Soy granules
   Corn germ, rice bran, or oat bran ‡
   Crushed nuts
   Roasted ground sprouted grains such as rye, triticale
(a wheat-rye hybrid), or buckwheat   2, 3
4.   Can't eat Wheaties? Try one of the alternative
flaked grains (free of salt, sugar, and additives) that
include corn, rye, triticale, barley, and even pinto
bean and soy flakes.   2, 3
5.   Sprouting may help you tolerate wheat. To make
sprouted wheat, place 1 cup whole wheat berries in a
jar; cover with water. Cover with nylon net and
secure with rubber band. Soak. Drain after twenty-
four hours. Place jar on side. Rinse and drain twice
daily, letting the berries sit until they sprout. Harvest
when "tail" is as long as the berry. (Use same method
with other grains such as rye and triticale.*) Allow
about three days.   2, 3
6.   Replace 1 tablespoon wheat flour used as a
thickener with 1½ teaspoons cornstarch, arrowroot, or
potato starch, tapioca flour, rice flour, or rye flour.†
Also see item 8 under Alternatives to Eggs.   2, 3
7.   Make a wheat-free substitute for your usual
pancake mix by combining 1 cup bean flour (lentil,
chick-pea, or soy) and 1 cup tapioca flour and 2

‡ Avoid regular bran. It is derived from wheat. A good substitute is Quaker Oats
   Company's new oat bran, available at health food stores.

* Sprouts can replace the wheat, sweetener, and eggs in dessert doughs if you
   grind them into a paste and correct their stickiness with an alternate flour such
   as rye or rice polish. Result is unconventional but uncannily sweet, heavy but
   dense and chewy. A recipe that eliminates these and yeast and milk as well? See
   Unbaked Christmas Cookies (p. 000).

† Artichoke flour and water chestnut flour are also useful. So is chick-pea or lima
   bean flour.

teaspoons allergen-free baking powder. Add 1
tablespoon oil and enough milk substitute for right
consistency. Make as you would wheat pancakes.   2, 3
8.   Make a high protein cake mix that's wheat-free,
by combining: 1½ cups soy flour or buckwheat flour, 1
cup arrowroot powder, ½ cup carob powder, and 3
teaspoons baking powder. Use to replace flour and
baking powder in corn bread, cupcake, and cake
recipes. Results will be light but on the crumbly side.   2, 3
9.   What else replaces wheat? Bean flour. It's gluten-
free and heavier than wheat but higher in protein. To
make your own, soak any dried bean overnight, drain,
and dry and grind a few at a time in a grain mill, food
mill, or in a processor or blender ° to convert into a
fine flour. If cracked beans are available, these are
easier to process than whole.   1, 2, 3

Note: Use 1 cup any alternative to replace 1 cup of wheat, unless
otherwise directed.

Alternatives to Corn

If you're allergic to corn. . .

                                                                  Sources
1.   Instead of corn flour, try any potato flour, soy
flour, or rice flour.   2, 3
2.   Instead of cornmeal, try soy grits or soy granules,
or grind raw brown rice or uncooked hot cereal in the
blender until mealy in texture.   2, 3
3.   Try millet, a small seeded grain with a nutty taste
somewhere between corn and wild rice. It's more
nutritious than corn, more readily digested, and rich
in vitamins, minerals, and protein. (NOTE: Millet
belongs to the cereal family, too. Watch for reactions
if you are very grain sensitive.)

° Check manufacturer's directions to make sure this is within your machine's
powers.

Instead of cornstarch:

1. Substitute potato starch, a thickener which is made from the liquid that remains after the potato flour has been made. It has a texture like cornstarch and makes a good thickener for puddings. For people who are allergic to wheat flour or cornstarch, potato starch is especially useful. Or try potato flour. It's made from potatoes that have been peeled, cooked, mashed, dried, and milled. It has the consistency of wheat flour and can be used to add extra flavor to bread, rolls, cookies, etc. It has about five times as much iron and four times as much potassium as whole-wheat flour, but slightly less calcium. It also contains vitamin C, a nutrient not found in whole-wheat flour.   *1, 2, 3*
2. Use arrowroot or tapioca flour, both starches that swell to form a gel when mixed with liquid and heated. Tapioca comes from the roots of the cassava plant and arrowroot from the tuberous roots of the maranta plant or its relatives.   *1, 2, 3*
3. Another analog for cornstarch is algin powder. Algin is a sea vegetable by-product used primarily in fruit desserts such as gelatins, sauces, and sherbets. It improves whipping quality and viscosity when boiled or used to whip cream. It is often used to thicken cooked food just before serving, since prolonged heating affects its jelling qualities. One teaspoon to 1 tablespoon per cup of water produces jelling of various strengths. Dissolve in liquid half an hour before using. Specific directions are given in recipes using algin. It adds fiber but few calories to low-fiber foods. Algin may be used in place of agar (kanten).   *2, 3*
4. Agar is a highly nutritious sea vegetable gelatin which can be used anywhere plain gelatin is used, and anywhere gelatin is used as a thickening agent instead of cornstarch. Agar has been used for 400 years in cooking. Unlike either cornstarch or gelatin, it is rich in all the health-boosting minerals, especially iodine and calcium. It is readily digested and has a very low

potential as an allergen. It is also known as kanten and
is available in bar form or granular flakes. All health
food stores carry it.   *2, 3*
5.   What else makes sauces and desserts thick?
Whipped fruit. Pureeing any fruit in the blender will
thicken it. If canned or frozen, drain the fruit. If dried,
soak in water and puree with soaking juices.   *1*

Note: Use 1 tablespoon cornstarch substitute to
replace 1 tablespoon of cornmeal, corn flour, or
cornstarch, unless otherwise specified.   *1, 2*

Alternatives to Chocolate

If you're allergic to chocolate or cocoa:

Sources

1.   Carob powder is the best substitute. It looks and
tastes like cocoa and chocolate but is unrelated. Carob
is derived from the dried bean pods of a subtropical
tree of the locust family. It is also in the legume family
so if you are sensitive to peas, beans, and the like, you
may be bothered by carob. Naturally sweet, high in
nutrients, and caffeine-free, it is available as an
unsweetened powder, unsweetened drops and chips,
and for blocks and bars with or without sugar. But
dark and light carob syrup can sometimes be found as
well and makes a nice corn syrup substitute. As a
powder, carob can be used like cocoa in baking and
beverages or with milk or nut milks. In a solid form it
can be used as a chocolate substitute. Adding coconut
oil or a tolerated nut oil to melted carob makes it

softer and tastier, or use a teaspoon of lecithin
granules for smoother results.°

Replace 1 tablespoon cocoa powder, with 1
tablespoon carob powder.

Replace 1 ounce of melted chocolate, with 3
tablespoons carob powder and 1½ teaspoons oil. Heat
and blend until smooth, or blend 3 tablespoons milk or
water with 3 tablespoons carob powder.

Replace 1 cup of hot chocolate or cocoa, with 1 cup
of milk blended with 1 tablespoon carob powder
sweetened to taste.   *1, 2, 3*

2.   Use diced dates, figs, or sugar-free carob chips to
replace chocolate chips.   *2, 3*

3.   Instead of ½ cup cocoa powder in baked goods
such as chocolate cookies and cupcakes, use a
combination of ¼ cup each decaffeinated instant
coffee powder, Postum or an herb coffee substitute
(such as Pero or Cafix), plus ¼ cup honey. Omit sugar.   *2, 3*

4.   Use blackstrap molasses in place of bittersweet
chocolate. It's rich in potassium, iron, and calcium.   *2, 3*

5.   Use natural sugar-free malt powder or dark
roasted chicory (an herb coffee substitute) in place of
cocoa, or malt syrup in place of melted chocolate to
add a chocolate color to baked goods.   *2, 3*

6.   Sorghum, light molasses, and maple syrup may be
used in place of chocolate syrup.   *2, 3*

Note: Use 1 tablespoon chocolate substitute to replace chocolate or
cocoa, unless otherwise specified.

Alternatives to Soybeans

If you are allergic to soybeans. . .

                                                            Sources

1.   Try other nut and vegetable oils and unsalted
butter in place of soy oil and soybean margarines.   *1, 2*

° For complete details on carob, read the author's *The Carob Way to Health*,
Warner Books, 1982.

2.   Use any other special B-vitamin–rich flour such as
rice flour, rice polish, or millet flour in place of soy
flour.   *2, 3*
3.   Use wheat germ, oat bran, or corn germ in place
of soy granules or soy lecithin.   *2, 3*
4.   Use other roasted nuts and beans such as peanuts
or chick-peas in place of roasted soybeans.   *1, 2, 3*
5.   Use dairy milk and cream or milk made from nuts
or vegetables in place of soy "dairy" foods. (See
chapter 5, Recipes, Milk and Cream Substitutes.)   *1*
6.   Use lecithin derived from seeds, vegetables, or egg
yolk. Liquid soy lecithin may be replaced with any
vegetable or nut oil.   *2, 3*

Note: 1 tablespoon of any soy substitute replaces 1 tablespoon of
any soy ingredient, unless otherwise noted.

Alternatives to Eggs

Doing without Humpty Dumpty isn't easy! Eggs are served
in dozens of desserts. Egg yolks add flavor and richness, whole
eggs hold the product together. Egg whites beaten to hold air
bubbles add lightness to cakes, cookies, and puddings. Choose
an egg substitute with these ends in mind.

If you're allergic to eggs. . .

                                                                   Sources
1.   Replace 1 egg yolk with ½ teaspoon baking
powder, or 2 tablespoons flour.   *1*
2.   Replace 1 egg white with ½ teaspoon fat, 1
tablespoon baking powder, or 4 tablespoons flour.   *1*
3.   Replace 1 whole egg with ½ teaspoon baking
powder plus 2 tablespoons flour and ½ tablespoon oil,

or 2 tablespoons water plus 1 tablespoon oil and 2
tablespoons baking powder, or 2 tablespoons water
plus 2 teaspoons baking powder.   *1*
4.   Replace 1 whole egg with 2 teaspoons baking
powder for the first egg in cake recipes or recipes of
that type. Then use 1 teaspoon baking powder for
each egg after that.   *1*
5.   Replacing 1 or 2 eggs in moist baked goods and
cookies with apple, other fruit sauce, or mashed
banana will supply cohesiveness and chewiness. So
will adding sweeteners and cooked starchy vegetable
purees, pureed cottage cheese, or tofu or nut butter.   *1, 2*
6.   Replace 1 egg in baking with 2 tablespoons
whole-wheat flour, ½ teaspoon baking powder, and 2
tablespoons milk, water, or fruit juice; 1 teaspoon
baking powder or substitute (see Baking Yeast) will
provide lightness but not body or stickiness.   *1*
7.   Replace 1 egg in puddings with gelatin, about 1
tablespoon per 2 cups liquid. Soak gelatin in ¼ cup
cold liquid. Stir into hot liquid until dissolved. Cool
and use to thicken.   *1*
8.   Replace 1 egg with 1 tablespoon lecithin granules
as a binder and emulsifier in breads. Or use 2
tablespoons agar plus 2 tablespoons flaxseed simmered
in 1 cup water for 5 minutes. This amount will thicken
2 cups of cooked grain in rice pudding–type desserts
using at least ½ cup liquid.   *1, 2*
9.   Replace an egg used as a binder or jelling agent
with ½ teaspoon algin powder dissolved in ½ cup
liquid.   *2, 3*
10.   Replace 1 beaten egg used to emulsify or bind
with 1 teaspoon nut butter plus enough water to equal
the consistency of the beaten egg, or 4 tablespoons nut
butter plus 2 tablespoons lemon juice, or 1 part soy
flour and 2 parts water. Mix, blend, and heat. Let cool.   *2, 3*
11.   Replace an egg used as leavening agent by
increasing baking powder by 1 teaspoon for each
omitted egg, or substitute ½ teaspoon arrowroot plus
¼ teaspoon baking soda for 1 egg.   *1, 2, 3*

Alternatives to Nuts

If you're allergic to nuts. . .

Sources

1.   Shell, crush, and/or dice any of the following:
     roasted chestnuts
     water chestnuts
     grape-nuts or other nonpresweetened dry cereal
     unsalted roasted soybeans
     nuts and sugar-free granola
     toasted rolled oats
     toasted sprouts
     Use in place of cashews, peanuts, or almonds, where
     appropriate. All of the above are lower in calories
     than nuts and slightly sweeter in most cases.   *1, 2, 3*
2.   Instead of ground nuts, use:
     oat bran °   *2, 3*
     rice bran and wheat bran
     corn germ and wheat germ   *2, 3*
     soy grits, soy granules
     blender-ground granola, or any crushed
     unsweetened dry cereal flake   *1, 2*
     any combination of Dessert Sprinkles (see chapter 5,
     Recipes, p. 83) compatible with other flavors in your
     recipe (may be pretoasted to intensify taste)
3.   Instead of nuts, oil, and nut butter:
     Switch to vegetable oils and health margarines.
     Health food stores carry the less refined preservative-
     free brands.   *1, 2, 3*
     Try less common oils such as hazelnut, walnut, and
     fruity olive. These may be tolerated even if peanut oil
     and sunflower seed oils are not.   *2, 3*
     If you are not corn intolerant, corn germ oil is a

° Produces a 10 percent greater reduction in cholesterol than ordinary fibers,
 according to the *American Journal of Clinical Nutrition*, 1981. Look for Quaker
 Oats Company's hot cereal called Mother's Oat Bran at health food stores and
 some supermarkets.

taste treat and is nutritionally superior to wheat germ
oil, and tastier than ordinary corn oil.   2, 3

In place of peanut butter? Try the other butters
made from nuts—almond butter; cashew; sesame;
sunflower. To reduce the price and raise protein,
mineral, and B-vitamin content, make a fifty-fifty
blended butter using 1 cup of toasted nutritional yeast
and 1 cup of nut butter. Repackage in a margarine tub
and refrigerate. Use in place of peanut butter or any
nut butter for snacks and cooking.   2, 3

4.   What else makes cookies and candies seem nutty?
Date chips, carob dots, crushed banana flakes, dried
fruit. All add nutlike texture if not taste to baked
goods.   2, 3

Note: Use 1 tablespoon of nut oil substitute for each tablespoon of
nuts, nut oil, or nut butter.

Alternatives to Citrus

If you're allergic to citrus. . .

                                                                            Sources

1.   Instead of oranges or orange juice try the fruit and
the juice of papaya, mango, passionfruit, persimmons.
In addition to vitamin C, they provide plenty of
vitamin A.   1, 2

2.   In place of dried orange or lemon peel ("zest") use
grated ginger, dried lemon verbena, lemon balm,
limeflower, or orange mint herbs. Consult your local
herb supplier for other citrusy-flavored suggestions.   2, 3

3.   If oranges are out you may still tolerate orange

water. If not, try rosewater when orange juice or
orange juice concentrate is called for. Or switch to a
natural extract such as wild cherry or wintergreen
extract. The Bickford brand—sold in health and food
stores—has these plus eighteen more.   2, 3

Note: Use 1 tablespoon orange juice substitute—liquid, dried, or
solid—to replace 1 tablespoon orange juice, orange, or other citrus.

Alternatives to Baking Yeast

If you are allergic to baking yeast. . .

                                                                    Sources

1.   Try baking powder. Unless labels tell you
otherwise, most baking powder contains unhealthy
aluminum compounds, lots of salt, and traces of corn.
Look or ask for low-sodium brands that are corn- and
aluminum-free.°   2, 3
2.   Make your own cornstarch-free, salt-free,
aluminum-free baking powder by combining 1 cup
potassium bicarbonate, 2 cups cream of tartar, and 2
cups arrowroot powder. Use in place of regular baking
powder.   2, 3
3.   There are even substitutes for substitutes. If you

° What's the difference between baking powder and baking soda? Baking soda
is an alkali. When combined with an acid, it gives off carbon dioxide, which
causes muffins, breads, and pancakes to rise. Unless there is an acid (either
sourdough starter or acid-type fruits) in your ingredients, the baking soda won't
work and you won't get any leavening. Commercial baking powders are usually
double-acting and effervesce both when the liquid is added and when ingredients are heated.

can't find item 1 above and don't want to do item 2,
make these substitutions:

1 teaspoon baking powder = ¼ teaspoon baking
soda and ½ teaspoon cream of tartar, *or* ¼ teaspoon
baking soda and ½ cup buttermilk, *or* ¼ teaspoon
baking soda and ⅓ cup molasses, honey, or homemade
liquid sweetener (see chapter 5, Recipes, Homemade
Sugars, Sweeteners, and Syrups)   *1*

4.   What else makes baked goods light? Adding
beaten eggs, or separating the eggs before adding in a
recipe, whipping the whites until stiff, or sifting dry
ingredients before adding to the liquid in a recipe.
Also see Alternatives to Eggs.   *1*

5.   Avoid sourdough starters as yeast alternatives.
They contain yeast as a natural ingredient derived
from airborne yeast spores.

Note: Use 4 teaspoons baking powder or baking powder substitute
to equal 1 tablespoon baking yeast. Baking powder and its substitutes can be used even with gluten-free flours.

Alternatives to Spices, Artificial Colors and Flavors

If you're allergic to common spices and extracts . . .

Sources

1.   Try coriander, cassia, cardamom, grated orange or
lemon peel. In fact, anything that makes a tasty cup of
tea can be a nice spice substitute. Experiment with
dried herbs. Examples? Blueberry, hyssop, balm,
woodruff, clover, chamomile, rose hip, anise, and
fennel.   *1, 2, 3*

2.   Instead of vanilla extract, substitute rose water,
orange water, oil of peppermint, or almond oil.
Nothing tastes just like vanilla bean, but the herb
woodruff comes close. Nearly odorless when fresh,
drying brings forth sweet, delicate vanillalike
fragrance. It also makes a nice cup of tea.   2, 3

If you're allergic to artificial colors and flavors . . .

3.   Instead of the artificial food dyes:
Green or pistachio °—use liquid chlorophyll or
spinulina sea vegetable powder.   2, 3
Red, pink—use beet juice
Caramel, chocolate or brown—use strong herb coffee
(Pero, Postum, Cafix)
Lavender—use blueberries or purple grapes
Orange—use carrot juice
Yellow—use pineapple juice
Brown—use apple juice
Purple—use grape juice
Other colors—use a combination of juices   2, 3
4.   Instead of artificially colored and flavored gelatin,
substitute plain gelatin and undiluted or partially
diluted fruit juice concentrates.

Note: How much of an alternative to use for a spice, dye, or flavor
allergen? Let your taste be your guide.

° Pistachio ice cream isn't green, thanks to pistachios. Although shelled pistachios
  have a greenish tinge on the outside and yellow meat within, it is in imitation of
  the green that the dye is added. Ditto for most peppermint stick ice cream. Red
  dye is what makes that distinctive color. Natural food colors are manufactured
  by Sorbee International, Philadelphia, PA 19115. (See mail order sources.)

III. 25 Allergy-Safe Substitutes

INSTEAD OF:

TRY:

1. Caramels or fudge — Frozen grapes (Thaw 15 minutes before eating.)

2. M & M's — Frozen raisins or currants (Thaw slightly.)

3. Doublemint gum — Soak whole wheat berries in double-strength mint tea overnight. Drain and chew.

4. French vanilla ice cream — Overripe bananas (Peel, freeze, half thaw, and munch.)

5. Hershey's Kisses — Chocolate-Free chocolate chips (chapter II, p. 49, item 2)

6. Life Savers — Any spicy herb tea frozen in mini ice-cube trays. Add a mint leaf or lemon peel before freezing. Store a sack of assorted flavors as allergic snack-attack stoppers.

7.	Dry roasted peanuts	No-Nut Granola (p. 96)
8.	Peach sherbet	Ripe frozen nectarines slightly thawed
9.	Frozen Snickers bars	Chilled Feast of Yeast Fudge (p. 160)
10.	Potato chips	Banana Ruffles (p. 163)
11.	Creamsicles	Peeled bananas on a stick, rolled in maple syrup and nuts, and frozen
12.	Salted peanuts	Pseudo Peanuts (p. 164)
13.	Marshmallows	Mix stiffly beaten egg whites with milk powder or arrowroot, drop by spoonfuls on cookie sheet, and dry in a 200°F oven for 30 minutes.
14.	Granola breakfast bars	Mix 2 cups homemade dry cereal (pp. 94–97) with 2 eggs. Bake in cake pan at 350°F until firm.
15.	Gumdrops	Dried persimmons or dried pitted cherries °
16.	Sugar cubes	Sugar Cubes (recipe p. 158)
17.	Candied ginger	Vermont Candied Ginger (p. 156)
18.	Charms	Diced dried bananas or honey-dried pineapple †
19.	Popcorn	Popped wheat. Feed whole wheat or rye berries into hot air corn popper. (They won't explode but they expand into a toasty sweet snack.)
20.	Fruit-flavored chewing gum	Raspberry "Chewing Gum" (p. 161)
21.	Grape-Nuts cereal	Sprouted oven-toasted wheat, rye, or alfalfa

° Available from Tokunaga Farms, 12019 Highland Avenue, Selma, CA 93662.
† Sold at health food stores and gourmet shops.

22.	Tums	Sun-dried papaya (contains the natural digestive enzyme papain)
23.	Yoo-Hoo soda	Cold carob cocoa (see chapter II, p. 49)
24.	Licorice breath fresheners	Fennel seed can be chewed like gum. Ditto anise.
25.	Butter Buds (the commercial butter-free butter substitute)	Pollen granules (They taste like honey, melt like butter when hot, and provide lots of allergy-fighting amino acids.)

IV. 50 Cooking Tips
for the Allergic

1. Vitamin C can prevent peeled bananas and apples from turning brown. Crush half a C tablet, add to cool water, immerse fruits. Take the other half of the C tablet yourself. Research indicates that 500 milligrams of vitamin C can help fight food allergy symptoms for up to six hours.

2. Make your own pumpkin pie spice. Combine 8 parts cinnamon powder, 2 parts ground ginger, 1 part ground cloves. Mix the spices together and store in a jar to use as needed.

Not having pie? Put a teaspoon into a cup of boiling water and have a no-caffeine, counterfeit cup of Constant Comment.

3. Perrier pancakes? Using sparkling water in place of juice or milk not only spares you allergies for breakfast, it makes super-light pancakes and waffles. Perrier is a good source of calcium.

4. How to make dry cereal taste sweeter and crispier without adding sugar? Toast it 10 minutes in a 325°F oven.

5. Muffins? Don't make a batch of muffins. Make one big one by baking all your batter in a fluted bundt cake pan.

6. Is there a chemically sensitive chef in the kitchen? Next time you make vanilla milk shakes save some of that vanilla extract for the paint bucket. One teaspoon will deodorize a whole gallon of latex.

7. Something hot that's not highly allergenic and is caffeine-free? Try ½ cup hot water with ½ cup any permitted fruit juice.

8. How can you make whipped honey in a hurry? Drip the honey into a blender set on low speed. Gradually increase blender speed as you continue to slowly pour in the honey until it thickens. Stop when the blender sounds as if it might be straining. If the honey needs further thickening, refrigerate. For a richer spread, add some butter and grated orange rind. Beat until fluffy. Refrigerate.

9. Orange juice off limits? Papaya's a better breakfast juice anyway. Four ounces gives you 51 milligrams of vitamin C, only 60 calories, and more vitamin A—2,500 units—than any other juice except carrot. Try it over cereal instead of milk.

10. What's an allergy-safe substitute for caffeinated black tea? Try vitamin C–rich raspberry or strawberry leaves tea.

11. A pinch of cream of tartar turns ordinary milk into unordinary buttermilk (unordinary because store-bought has up to 257 milligrams of sodium per cup; homemade has half that). Salt is a stress factor.

12. Can't eat birthday cake? Cut a cake-size hunk out of a big sweet melon. Lay it flat on a plate and decorate with candles. Optional: Frost with Milk-Free Quick Whipped Topping (see p. 150).

13. Allergic to peppermint tea? Use cloves. Brew tea with 1 teaspoon per cup of boiling water. Simmer 15 minutes, steep, and strain. Save what's left for a chemical-free mouthwash. Cloves have 50 percent more vitamin C than cinnamon or allspice.

14. Is your cheesecake always pale-faced? Do what commercial bakeries do—run it briefly under the broiler for a fast browning.

15. White bread may contain eight of the top twelve allergens. But it's a great preservative. Keep a slice in your jar of homemade sugar (page 79) or date sugar to prevent caking.

16. Next-best-thing-department: What tastes just like the New England pie variety of pumpkin you're allergic to? The roasted chestnuts you aren't.

17. What's better than Jell-O straight up? Shredded Jell-O. It's simple. Refrigerate or freeze any gelatin dessert until *very* firm, force through a potato ricer, divide into individual dishes, and serve.

18. Allergic to honey? Drop a few dried cherries in your cup of tea instead.

19. Are all oils off limits? Brown foods under the broiler instead of with oil in a skillet. Baste with juice (such as pineapple or papaya) to prevent drying out.

20. Citrus peels are natural air fresheners. The citrus oils released by the heat will permeate your pantry with their pungency.

21. Lots of allergy-arousing corn syrup and refined sugar help turn whipped eggs into sturdy meringues. But so does white vinegar or cream of tartar. Use ¼ teaspoon of either for every 3 whites.

22. Sugar-free alternative to graham cracker piecrusts? Crushed Grape-Nuts (or a similar cereal) with apple juice and cinnamon.

23. How to prevent high-fiber flops when you're baking breads with low-gluten wheat-free flours? Add 1 tablespoon lemon juice or mild vinegar for every 2½ cups flour when you're combining the liquid ingredients. It improves the elasticity of the gluten, which helps baked goods rise better and higher.

24. Poppy seed puts crunch in your batters and piecrusts even if nuts are a no-no. So does raw millet.

25. Fallen soufflé? Simmer ½ cup heavy cream for 5 minutes. Pour over your crestfallen creation, cover loosely with foil, place dish in a pan of warm water, and reheat in a preheated 350° oven until it is risen again and warm. As the soufflé absorbs the cream, it repuffs. Try it on both allergy-free and ordinary soufflés.

26. Allergic to butter and the milk it contains? Spread your toast while it's still hot with jam or honey or something you *can* have and you'll never notice the omission.

27. How to get salt to stick to unbuttered, air-popped corn or corn substitutes? Sprinkle it with a very light mist of water from a plant mister. The salt will stick and the corn stays crunchy.

28. Only semiallergic to butter? You can cut it down, not out, if you brown it first. This reduces volume and concentrates flavor so you use 50 percent less.

29. Soft-style tofu won't do what firm tofu does. If you've got the former, here's how to turn it into the latter. Cut into cubes and place on a towel. Place another towel on top. Place a cookie sheet or cutting board over all and add about three pounds of weight evenly distributed. Let stand 10 minutes.

30. Will anything ever replace the taste of Mom's apple pie crust, if you can't have wheat? Sure. Cheese. Before removing your apple pie (with its wheat-free crust) from the oven, sprinkle the top with ½ cup grated Cheddar cheese. It melts in a second. (If you *can* eat wheat, sprinkle cheese on the bottom crust before adding filling. Bake as specified.)

31. Adding ½ cup potato flour to replace 1 cup wheat flour reduces your exposure to grain allergens, improves the flavor of baked goods, and also adds allergy-reductive ascorbic acid.

32. Got some overripe peaches? Make additive-free Chinese duck sauce. Peel peaches; puree in processor or blender with a dash of soy sauce, vinegar, or lemon juice to taste. Refrigerate.

33. Lots of peas will sweeten up soup. Lots of onions will do the same for spaghetti sauce.

34. Cinnamon is not forever. To keep fresher longer, refrigerate. The same goes for ginger and cloves. Vanilla beans keep best stored side by side with a humidifying cake (tobacco stores sell them) that can be moistened as needed, says the trade journal *Whole Foods*.

35. Want a perfect brown-not-burned piecrust every time, even if you're cooking with wheat flour substitutes? Place a

1½-inch-wide strip of foil around crust; bake as recipe indicates. Remove foil last 15 minutes of baking.

36. Bad water makes bad desserts. Detoxify the water and improve your tolerance to some of the allergy-aggravating chemicals it contains. New portable strawlike gadgets that purify water sell for less than fifteen dollars and are designed so that harmful water clogs the filters and will not pass through. The straw is reusable until its purification capacity is exhausted.

37. Bananas can be your best friend if you're allergic to citrus, and they keep three to four days longer if refrigerated. Skins turn black, but insides remain firm, tasty. Bananas, when ripe, owe their taste to over 150 substances, says the Natural Food and Farming Association. The specks on a banana peel are called sugar spots.

38. "Caramel flavor" is just allergy-triggering burnt sugar, unless you make it yourself by toasting and grinding healthy roast chicory (all natural food stores stock this coffee grain substitute).

39. Avoiding milk? Avoid so-called nondairy creamers, too. Besides the fact that they contain more saturated fat than whole milk does, just as many calories, plus corn sugar, they also contain sodium caseinate, which is derived from cow's milk.

40. Can't have spice *in* your cookies? Have it under them. Sprinkle pineapple sage leaves on a cookie sheet, bake cookies on top. Tasty with sage tea.

41. Can't have soy flour? Make sweet potato flour. Wash and peel raw sweet potatoes, slice them cross-wise into ¼-inch-thick pieces, and dry until crispy. (In an electric dehydrator set at 120°F; this takes 16 hours.) When dry, grind in blender or processor. Sweet potatoes rank with spinach and carrots as one of the richest sources of vitamin A.

42. Allergic to most common fruits? To satisfy your uncommon craving for jams and jellies, check stores for offbeat grape jelly from the South—sapodilla plum, scuppernong, or muscadine—or Florida's jellies made from acerola (the Barbados cherry, rich in vitamin C) and carissa (the Natal plum), or the pyracantha jelly of Texas, or Hawaii's papaya preserves and guava jelly.

43. Like your milk-free oatmeal really piping hot on cold mornings? Instead of cold soy milk, stir in ⅓ cup toasted soy powder per serving and a little extra water as you cook it. Result? Creamy, smooth cereal that stays hot to the bottom of the bowl.

44. Allergic to air fresheners? Use eucalyptus in the kitchen. The branches are decorative, last forever, and rubbing the leaves intensifies the odor. (Most floral shops stock them.)

45. Can't eat sherbet? Cut 3 persimmons in half. Place a piece of wax paper over cut edge and freeze 2 hours. Let thaw for 15 minutes. Serves 3.

46. Store-bought jam has 55 calories a tablespoon. This one gives you 10: Puree soft blueberries with a squirt of lemon juice. Refrigerate. It's ready to spread in an hour.

47. For a fast sugar-free dessert, bruised pears can be pared, poached in red wine, and chilled.

48. What contains vitamin C besides ordinary corn-based vitamin C tablets? Per 100 grams, dried coriander leaf has 567 milligrams, garden cress has 69 milligrams, and dried rosemary has 61 milligrams.

49. Are you wheat allergic? Here's a no-cook counterfeit shortcake: Saturate a health-food-store bought rice cake with hot milk. Top with honey-sweetened strawberries. Repeat layers three times. Top with milk-free Tofu Half 'n' Half (page 77).

50. Sugar depletes your iron reserves. Raisin juice builds it up. To make it, soak one pound of golden or black raisins overnight in hot water or hot herb tea. Strain. Add a teaspoon of lemon juice and puree liquid with a tablespoon of the soaked raisins.

V. Recipes

___

Milk and Cream Substitutes

Milk Substitutes

No milk or butterfat
No sugar
No corn
No wheat
No spice

Allergy Milk # 1

Use as you would conventional cow's milk.
3 cups soy milk or other milk substitute
2 cups freshly grated coconut

1. In a saucepan, combine soy milk or other milk substitute and grated coconut.

2. Bring the milk to a boil, remove the pan from the heat, and let the mixture stand at room temperature for 30 minutes.

3. Pour the mixture through damp cheesecloth, squeezing out all the liquid.

Makes 3 cups; about 100 calories per cup

Options: 1. Substitute real milk for milk substitute. 2. Go on a blender bender. Have a glass for a breakfast on the run.

Did you know that a recent study in the *British Medical Journal* revealed that young women who either skipped breakfast or had only coffee experienced a much greater incidence of gallstones than young women who ate a morning meal? Researchers concluded that long intervals between meals "might increase the risk of gallstone formation."

No soy
No milk
No corn
No wheat
No sugar
No spice

Allergy Milk #2

A presweetened dairy milk substitute.
½ cup hulled sesame seed
3 cups mineral water
4 pitted dates

1. Combine all ingredients in blender or processor until smooth.

2. Strain. Refrigerate. No cooking needed.

Options: 1. Use soy milk in place of water for a richer version. 2. Substitute 4 tablespoons any homemade dry sugar (see Homemade Sugars, Sweeteners, and Syrups) for dried dates.

Makes 3 cups; 100 calories per cup

Did you know that soy milk has almost the same amount of protein contained in regular whole milk and a similar taste yet lacks most of the cholesterol and has only 74 calories per cup (about half the amount you get from cow's milk)?

No milk
No soy
No corn
No spice
No sugar

Wheat Milk

2 cups sprouted wheat (see Options)
3 cups water or noncarbonated spring water

Combine ingredients in blender or food processor until smooth and thick.

Options: 1. For "Chocolate" Wheat Milk blend in ½ to 1 level teaspoon carob powder per cup. 2. Use sprouted rye or triticale if you have a wheat allergy. Available at some health food stores. 3. Sprouted wheat is sweet, but if it's not sweet enough for you, add honey to taste.

Makes 1 quart; 60 calories per cup

Did you know that the sodium content of mineral water varies depending on the source? Bottled water may have as little as 2.9 milligrams of sodium per liter (about 1 quart) or as much as 1,700 milligrams. To find out what you're getting, write (enclose a self-addressed, stamped envelope) to: International Bottled Water Association, Suite 1116, 1010 Vermont Avenue, N.W., Washington, D.C. 20005.

No milk
No soy
No corn
No wheat
No refined sugar
No spices

Dessert Milk #1

Use this low-calorie, no-cholesterol "plant" milk just as you would dairy milk.

6 medium zucchini
Water to cover
2 tablespoons any homemade dry sugar (see pp. 79–84)

1. Wash zucchini; dice.

2. Put squash into a blender container, 1 cup at a time; cover with water. Puree.

3. Strain. To thicken, reduce water. To thin, increase water.

Options: 1. Use yellow summer squash in place of zucchini. 2. Use 1 tablespoon light molasses or maple syrup in place of dry sweetener.

Makes 3 to 4 cups; about 25 calories per cup

Did you know that caramel flavor is just burnt sugar? You can make your own caramel-flavored milk naturally. Process one can of evaporated dairy or goat's milk for 10 minutes at 15 pounds of pressure. It's super for dessert baking.

No milk
No corn
No wheat
No refined sugar
No spices

Dessert Milk #2

Use as a dairy milk substitute.

1 cup dried soybeans
Water to cover plus 4 cups water
Honey to taste

1. Soak beans for 24 to 48 hours in enough water to cover. Change water twice daily.

2. Drain. Place soaked beans in a saucepan with 4 cups of water. Bring to a boil; simmer 1 hour, remove from heat, and let cool.

3. Pour into blender or processor. Process at a low speed until smooth. Strain. Sweeten to taste with honey.

Options: 1. Substitute cracked soybeans and reduce soaking time by 50 percent. 2. Replace 1 cup water in step 2 with 1 cup Almond Milk (p. 72) or coconut milk. For Vanilla Dessert Milk add ½ teaspoon pure vanilla extract. 3. To make a faster version, blend: 1 cup soy flour, 4 cups water in top of a double boiler. Let stand 2 hours. Place over hot water and bring the milk to a boil. Cook 20 minutes. Cool and strain. 4. Faster yet? Combine 1 cup soy powder with 3 cups water in a large saucepan. Whisk until well dissolved. Bring to a boil over high heat, stirring constantly. Lower heat and simmer for 3 minutes. Serve hot or cold. (Makes 3 cups.) 5. Use whole green soybeans (available from Walnut Acres, see Appendix B, Mail Order Sources) and you'll produce pea-green soybean milk!

Makes 3½ cups; 100 calories per cup

Did you know that soybeans are rich in B vitamins and protein, low in sodium, and high in all the other essential minerals?

No soy
No milk
No eggs
No refined sugar
No citrus
No spices

Fruit Cake Shake

Serve as a fake milk shake or use as a cooking milk. It's sweet enough to make extra sugar unnecessary.

*8 ounces apple juice or any fruity flavored herb beverage
   (available in health food stores)*
1 ripe banana
¼ cup diced pitted dates
1 cup water

1. Put all ingredients in blender and process until liquefied.

2. For thinner consistency, add more water or juice.

Options: 1. Substitute figs for dates. And before dicing, rub nut or seed oil on your knife or scissors, or sprinkle figs or dates with flour or arrowroot to prevent fruit from sticking together or to cutting surface. 2. Substitute water or unsweetened tea to reduce sweetness; ½ teaspoon kelp (salt substitute) adds extra calcium.

Makes 3 servings; 175 calories each

Did you know that Dacopa is a coffeelike herb powder derived from the dahlia flower? It's free of caffeine and has no bitter aftertaste. It's available from California Natural Products. No additives and only 4 calories per serving.

No milk
No corn
No wheat
No refined sugar

Almond Milk

4½ cups blanched almonds
4 cups water
3 tablespoons Fruit Fructose Paste (see p. 85) or 6 pitted dates

1. Put all ingredients in blender or processor and puree until smooth.

2. Strain. To thin, add more water.

Options: 1. Add ½ teaspoon nutritional yeast (if tolerated) per 16 ounces to improve vitamin B content. 2. Make "chocolate" milk by adding 1 teaspoon carob powder per cup. 3. Use cashews or pine nuts instead of almonds.

Makes slightly more than 1 quart; 150 calories per cup

Did you know that almonds contain large amounts of protein, vitamin B, potassium, and calcium? They are the essential ingredients in marzipan and are often recommended for nursing mothers as the most easily digestible of all the nuts.

No chocolate
No caffeine
No refined sugar

Copycat Cocoa

Use this hot as a cocoa substitute or cold as a chocolate milk taste-alike.

2 tablespoons light molasses
Pinch pumpkin pie spice (see item 2, p. 60)
2 cups skim or whole milk

1. Combine all ingredients together in a saucepan.

2. Heat gently.

3. Serve with a peppermint stick as a swizzle.

Note: For a milder drink, reduce the amount of spices or eliminate them completely.

Options: 1. Cool and serve with ice cubes as Iced Copycat Cocoa. 2. Freeze leftovers as ice cubes. Use as a hot weather hard candy substitute.

Makes 2 servings of 1 cup each; 100 calories each

Did you know that the caffeine and related stimulant theobromine in cocoa do a better job of getting you down than picking you up? According to Dr. Charles Ehret, a researcher at Argonne National Laboratory in Chicago, stimulating hot drinks for breakfast slow you down during the day and stir you up at night. If you've got to have something caffeinated, have it at 3:30 or 4:00 P.M. At that point, the effect is neutral: it neither advances nor delays the metabolic cycle. At other times, try Copycat Cocoa.

No milk
No refined sugar
No citrus
No spices

Watermelon "Milk" Punch

2 cups diced and seeded watermelon
1 cup fresh strawberries
1 cup milk substitute such as Dessert Milk #2

1. Combine all ingredients in a blender container or food processor and puree until smooth.

2. Serve in tall glasses over ice.

Options: 1. Use ¼ cup tofu pureed with ½ cup water in place of milk substitute. 2. Substitute raspberries for strawberries.

Makes 4 servings; about 90 calories each

Did you know that the usual 4- to 8-inch-long wedge of watermelon contains about 30 milligrams each of calcium and vitamin C, 2,510 units of vitamin A, 2.1 milligrams of iron, plus small quantities of protein and B vitamins, and only 93 calories? Watermelon seeds also contain a natural substance called cucubocitrin, which helps normalize blood pressure and speeds detoxification of your system.

Cream Substitutes

No milk or butter
No corn
No wheat
No nuts
No eggs
No soy
No refined sugar
No spices

Health Cream #1

Use this low–milkfat, no-cholesterol cream as a coffee light-ener or a cereal cream. Or serve over desserts.

1 cup skim milk powder
1 cup liquid milk
2 tablespoons safflower oil
Soy lecithin granules (optional)

1. Add ingredients to a blender container and blend at high speed.

2. Refrigerate before using.

Options: 1. Milk-free version—substitute powdered soy milk and liquid soy milk in same amounts as dairy milk. 2. Use nut or seed oil (such as peanut oil or sunflower seed oil) in place of safflower oil. 3. For thicker, richer consistency add 2 extra tablespoons powdered milk or powdered soy milk. 4. Add a dash of vanilla or 1 tablespoon honey to sweeten.

Makes 1 cup; 50 calories per tablespoon

Did you know that a pinch of cream of tartar will transform plain milk into buttermilk? But if raisins raise your hackles, skip them. Cream of tartar is made from raisins.

No milk or butterfat
No corn
No soy
No wheat
No spices
No eggs
No refined sugar

Health Cream #2

Use on cold cereals, gelatins, and fruit desserts.

2/3 cup chopped walnuts
2 cups of ice water, or 1 cup cold water plus 1 cup shaved ice

1. Blend ingredients in a blender or food processor until smooth. Chill.

2. To thin, add more water. To thicken, use more nuts.

Options: 1. For a richer cream use 1/3 cup each almonds and walnuts, plus 1 tablespoon honey. 2. For a sweeter Health Cream, add ½ teaspoon vanilla and 2 to 4 tablespoons any homemade sweetener (see Homemade Sugars, Sweeteners, and Syrups).

Makes 2½ cups; 40 calories per tablespoon

No milk
No wheat
No corn
No eggs
No refined sugar
No spices

Strawberry "Half and Half"

Serve cold over cooked fruits or plain cake.

½ cup soy powder (flour) (see Note)
4 tablespoons honey
1 cup water
Juice of 1 lemon
1 cup fresh strawberries, or ½ cup frozen, thawed, and drained

1. Process all ingredients in a blender or processor, adding additional water for thinner consistency.

2. Refrigerate.

Options: 1. Use protein powder in place of soy. 2. Use raspberries in place of strawberries. 3. Thicken with additional fruit, use as a frosting.

Makes about 2 cups; about 15 calories per tablespoon

Note: To improve flavor, spread soy powder in a shallow dry pan or skillet. Place in a preheated 300°F oven for 15 to 20 minutes and toast (stirring once) until lightly browned and pungent.

Did you know you can use citrus rind—lemon, orange or grapefruit—to remove hard-water marks from dishes and glassware? Rub marks with rind that has been dipped in hot water.

No milk or butterfat
No wheat
No corn
No spices
No refined sugar

Tofu "Half and Half"

8 ounces tofu
8 ounces water
Honey to taste

1. Puree tofu and water in a blender or food processor until consistency is creamy.

2. Add more water to thin, more tofu to thicken. Add a little honey to sweeten.

Options: 1. For Coconut Tofu "Half and Half" substitute store-bought coconut milk for water or use homemade (see Allergy Milk # 1).

Makes 2 cups; about 20 calories per tablespoon

Did you know that coconut adds protein, potassium, phosphorus, magnesium, and iodine to your diet? It is also lower in fat than most other nuts.

No milk or butterfats
No refined sugars
No wheat
No corn
No spices

Sunflower Seed "Sour Cream"

A great fruit salad dressing.

1 cup sunflower seed
½ cup sesame seed
2 cups water or more as needed

1. Grind together sunflower and sesame seeds in a coffee mill or nut grinder. Grind should be very fine.

2. Add enough water to reduce the mixture to the consistency of heavy cream, using either a blender or fork to stir.

3. Let the mixture sit 8 to 15 hours in a warm—70° to 80°F— room until it sours to desired consistency.

Options: 1. To intensify flavor, toast seeds (10 minutes on a cookie sheet in a 400°F oven). Stir twice before grinding. 2. For a sweeter version substitute apple juice for water.

Makes 2 cups; 75 calories per tablespoon

Did you know that according to Federal Trade Commission standards, "natural" foods may not contain artificial ingredients or be more than "minimally processed." But to call a food natural when it has been more than minimally processed, an advertiser can just identify the type of processing on the label—for example, *Natural but ultrapasteurized.*

Homemade Sugars, Sweeteners, and Syrups

Note: In the recipes that follow the term "fructose" refers to the major natural sugar that occurs in all fruits and vegetables in varying amounts. Commercial fructose is more highly refined than refined cane and beet sugar and is usually derived from corn, which leading allergists regard as the country's leading allergen.

Homemade Grain Sugars

No wheat
No corn
No citrus
No refined sugar
No nuts
No soy

Plain Grain Sugar

Oats are naturally sweet, but toasting makes them even sweeter—they're a fine sugar substitute.

2 cups "old-fashioned" rolled oats
1 cup rye flakes (see Options)
Water as needed
Cinnamon to taste
Mace (optional)

1. Preheat oven to 325°F.

2. Place oats and rye flakes in a colander. Dampen with water, drain well.

3. Lay out in a thin layer in a shallow baking pan or on a cookie sheet.

4. Place in oven to toast, stirring from time to time to avoid overbrowning, about 20 to 30 minutes. Sprinkle lightly with cinnamon and mace, if desired, for the final 5 minutes of toasting.

4. Cool. Then grind to powder in blender. Store in a tight container.

Options: 1. Can't buy rye? Try triticale flakes, soy flakes, or barley flakes instead. All are staples at well-stocked health food stores. 2. Grain Sugar may also be used as a coffee substitute. Add 1 teaspoon to a cup of boiling water and strain before using. 3. For Plain Grain Sugar Plus (a sweeter version), combine ½ cup Plain Grain Sugar with ½ cup maple syrup granules or date sugar.

Makes 3 cups; 100 calories each cup

No corn
No refined sugar
No soy
No citrus
No spices
No nuts

Wheat Sugar

Homemade malt from nonbarley.

4 cups whole wheat berries

1. Preheat oven to 300°F for 20 minutes. Then lower to 250°F.

2. Toast wheat berries in oven on ungreased baking sheet on lowest rack in oven for 1 hour or until they are medium brown and fragrant. Stir occasionally.

3. Grind to a powder in blender. Store in tightly covered canister or jar. May also be frozen in plastic bags.

Makes 8 cups; 50 calories per ½ cup

No corn
No citrus
No refined sugar
No soy

Fruit-Fiber Sugar

Use to sweeten hot and cold cereals and fruit desserts or use as a sprinkle.

2½ cups "old-fashioned" rolled oats
2 cups Grape-Nuts
½ cup rice flour
½ cup nonfat dry milk
1 teaspoon cinnamon
3 large apples, cored, peeled, and grated
2–3 tablespoons undiluted apple juice concentrate
1 teaspoon vanilla extract

1. Preheat oven to 275°F.

2. In a bowl combine all ingredients. Spread on a flat nonstick pan, spreading mixture into a thin layer.

3. Bake for about 45 minutes, or until mixture is dry.

4. Grind in blender until powdery. Store in airtight jar.

Options: 1. Substitute soy powder for milk powder. 2. Substitute frozen orange juice concentrate or bottled cherry juice concentrate for apple juice. 3. Omit grinding. Eat as a nut-free snack.

Makes 6 cups; 100 calories per cup

No refined sugar
No corn
No citrus
No soy

Mint Sugar

Store maple syrup granules, date sugar, or any homemade dry sugar in a glass jar with fresh mint leaves (peppermint, spearmint, etc.), dried mint leaves, or mint-flavored Life Savers. Use 2 fresh leaves, 1½ teaspoons dried leaves, or 2 Life Savers per cup of "sugar." Close jar tightly. To insure permeation of mint flavor and aroma stir sugar several times.

Makes 1 cup

Vanilla Sugar

1-2 vanilla beans
1 cup any homemade dry sugar

Bury 1 or 2 vanilla beans in a glass jar filled with store-bought or homemade dry sugar. Cut beans lengthwise to speed up flavorizing process. Fine quality vanilla beans will aromatize sugar for many months. So you can add more sugar as you use up supply.

Makes 1 cup

No refined sugar
No corn
No wheat
No spices

Peppermint Sugar

Use as you would any dry sugar. Sprinkle on cereal, buttered toast, and so on.

2 egg whites
1 tablespoon lemon juice
24 fresh mint leaves
Maple syrup granules

1. Combine egg whites and lemon juice and "paint" mint leaves, using a pastry brush.

2. Sprinkle leaves with maple granules.

3. Dry on a rack in a draft-free room until leaves are almost brittle. This may require 2 to 4 days.

4. Crush leaves to a fine powder or grind in a blender and store in a glass jar in a dry environment.

Makes ½ cup; 10 calories per tablespoon

Did you know that you can cut calories by replacing confectioners' sugar with noninstant skim milk powder?

Ginger Sugar

Use whenever a taste of both sugar and spice would be nice.

1 recipe Vermont Candied Ginger (see p. 156)

Crush with rolling pin or pulverize to a "sugar powder" in blender. Store in a jar.

Makes 1/3 cup

Dessert Sprinkles

Use 1 teaspoon or more per serving over hot cereal, cold cereal, buttered toast, pancakes, and so on. "Sprinkles" may be combined, i.e., wheat germ plus date sugar or toasted oats plus orange zest. Any ingredients may be toasted in a dry skillet, over surface heat, or on a cookie sheet in a 400°F oven until lightly browned. Stir and watch that sprinkles don't burn.

Unsweetened coconut, toasted or raw

Sprouted seeds or nuts, raw or lightly toasted and coarsely ground

Citrus zest (the dried, ground peel of organic oranges, kumquats, tangerines, lemons, etc.)

Toasted millet, sesame, chia (a poppy seed look-alike rich in B complex), caraway, or poppy seed

Crushed or ground granola or Grape-Nuts

Toasted rolled oats

Toasted crushed shredded wheat

Wheat germ, corn germ, or bran flakes, raw or toasted

Toasted plain puffed wheat or puffed rice

Date sugar or dry maple syrup granules

Pumpkin seed or sunflower seed ground into a meal, raw or toasted

Chopped unsalted peanuts

Finely diced dried fruit (papaya, apple, date, fig, apricot, raisin, etc.)

Soy granules

Bee pollen or lecithin granules

Lightly toasted nutritional yeast (heating improves flavor)

Sugar-free carob chips or carob "curls" grated off a carob block or bar

Any homemade dry sugar

Powdered herb tea leaves: aromatic blends with peppermint and chamomile, rose hips and cinnamon, lemon balm and alfalfa, alone or with any of the above sprinkles

Instant "mocha": Dry milk powder sifted with 1 part carob powder

Mock licorice: 2 teaspoons cinnamon, ½ teaspoon fennel seed, ½ teaspoon whole cloves ground in a seed mill and stirred into ¼ cup dry soy milk powder

Sweeteners

No wheat
No soy
No corn
No refined sugar
No citrus
No spices

Fruit Fructose Paste

A dried fruit sweetener.

1 cup chopped, pitted dried dates
½ cup water

1. Combine ingredients in a blender or processor container.

2. Puree until you have a smooth, creamy paste.

Options: 1. Dried dates are the sweetest of fruits, but another dried fruit (such as figs) may be substituted. 2. Use a mild herb tea in place of water.

Makes 1 cup; 50 calories per tablespoon

Did you know that resorting to a food allergen, such as sugar, to relieve fatigue only increases fatigue after the stimulation wears off? Instead, try a tea made from saffron, licorice root, or dandelion roots. All three support adrenal function and help neutralize the lactic acid accumulation in muscles that prevent your enzymes system from working as it should.

No wheat
No corn
No refined sugar
No soy
No spices

Fig Fructose

2 quarts unsweetened fig juice
Juice of 1 lemon

1. Combine juices in a deep heavy-bottom saucepan or canning kettle.

2. Boil until liquid is reduced to 50 percent of original volume and is syrupy (the more you boil the sweeter and more concentrated liquid becomes).

3. Store in refrigerator. Use as you would apple fructose.

Options: 1. Substitute 1 cup cherry, cranberry or grape juice for 1 cup fig juice. 2. Substitute juice of 1 lime or 1 small orange for lemon.

Makes 4 cups; 50 calories per tablespoon

Did you know figs are not a laxative themselves? Clinical ecologist Theron G. Randolph says it's the residue of sulfur dioxide and fumigants on commercial supermarket-purchased figs that causes the problem if you have food allergies. It's worth going organic. In addition, figs taste better than prunes and help to promote a healthy alkaline condition in the body which in turn promotes general good health. (An acid biochemical body climate usually accompanies illness. It also encourages bad habits like caffeine, alcohol, and nicotine abuse.)

No soy
No spices
No corn
No refined sugar

Apple Fructose

½ cup water
2 12-ounce cans undiluted apple juice concentrate

1. Combine water and juice in a deep, heavy pot. Set pot on asbestos pad to prevent scorching.

2. Bring juice to boil and continue to boil until juice is reduced to a thick syrup.

Options: 1. For Orange Fructose, substitute 2 12-ounce cans orange juice concentrate for apple juice. 2. Add 1 teaspoon lemon juice.

Note: Cooking with fruit concentrate is calorie conservative as well as healthy—2 tablespoons of the homemade apple fructose contains about 50 calories as compared to 120 calories for honey.

Makes about 1½ cups; 25 calories per tablespoon

Did you know that apples are rich in pectin and malic acid, two organic elements that aid the digestive process? They are also richer in vitamins A, B, and C than honey.

No refined sugar
No artificial colors
No corn
No wheat
No spices

Liquid Cherries

Use as a fruit-flavored sweetener.

1 lb. pitted cherries (sour as possible)
1½ cups water
2 tablespoons honey
1 tablespoon strained lime juice
1 tablespoon agar flakes

1. Combine the cherries and water in a saucepan. Bring to boil and simmer 15 minutes.

2. Line a colander with cheesecloth and place over a bowl. Pour the cherries and their liquid into the colander and let drain 30 minutes. Discard cherries, reserving the 1 cup liquid.

3. Add honey and lime juice to cherry liquid. Adjust sweetness to taste. Stir in agar flakes. Let rest 10 minutes, and stir again.

4. Bring mixture to boil in same saucepan, then cook over moderate heat for 10 minutes without stirring. Skim foam. Cool.

5. Pour into glass jar when cool. Refrigerate, tightly covered (and store in refrigerator).

Options: 1. Make a Cherry Sparkler—dilute 2 to 3 tablespoons syrup with 1 glass sparkling water. Serve over ice with twist of lime. Or use tap water and pour over ice. 2. Make Raspberry Honey—substitute 1 pound of raspberries for cherries.

Makes 1 cup syrup; 35 calories per tablespoon

Did you know that cherries and raspberries are good low-calorie sources of vitamin A and C, which keep your immune system healthy? Persons with a suppressed immune system may develop hypersensitivities to everything in their environment—chemicals, foods, dusts, molds, and pollens.

Syrups

No wheat
No corn
No citrus
No refined sugar
No spices

Simple Honey Syrup

½ cup raw unfiltered honey
4 cups cold water

1. Put honey and water in a saucepan. Boil until mixture is of a syrupy consistency.

2. Refrigerate.

Note: This sweetener is lower in calories, contains less natural sugar, and is less sticky than straight honey.

Options: 1. Add a pinch of lemon or orange peel. 2. For Spicy Honey Syrup, add ⅛ teaspoon each nutmeg and mace. 3. For Honey Vanilla Syrup, add ½ teaspoon vanilla extract. 4. For Simple Maple Syrup, substitute maple syrup for the honey. Makes 2 cups; 150 calories per cup

Allergic to cloves? Avoid vanillin which is manufactured from eugenol, the chief component of oil of cloves.

No corn
No wheat
No refined sugar
No spices

Did you know that even odors can trigger allergic reactions? Common kitchen offenders include fresh baked buckwheat flour, fried eggs, cooked vegetables, and ammonia fumes from cleaning products.

No refined sugar
No corn
No wheat
No spices
No citrus
No soy

5-Minute Maple Dribble

Dribble it over cakes or muffins while they're still warm.

1 cup maple syrup
1 tablespoon unsalted butter

1. Gently boil maple syrup with butter in deep pot (to prevent boilover) for 5 minutes.

2. Cool slightly.

Note: To increase saturation of syrup, pierce the cake top with a fork before pouring or dribbling.

Options: 1. For Apple Maple Dribble, add 1 tablespoon apple juice concentrate (undiluted) before boiling. 2. For Maple Cream Dribble, blend in 2 tablespoons blender-whipped tofu *after* boiling. Blender whip again to emulsify.

Makes 1 cup; 65 calories per tablespoon

Did you know the real harm in refined table sugar, says mega-vitamin therapist Dr. John Baron of Cleveland, is that "it is a chemical formula so concentrated it immediately affects pancreatic function within a half hour? Yet the human pancreas is unable to tolerate the bombardment of sugar. Sugar is as much an addiction as caffeine and nicotine."

No refined sugar
No corn
No wheat
No spices

Rice Syrup

Use in place of honey or corn syrup.

4 cups brown rice
12 cups water
2 cups crushed or finely chopped fresh sprouts (of any
*   tolerated grain, rice, rye, wheat, etc.) (see Options)*

1. Boil brown rice, covered, without salt in water for 45 minutes or until tender. Cool to 140°F (use a candy thermometer).

2. To the cooked rice add fresh sprouted grains. Blend the rice and sprouts.

3. Cover and keep in a warm place, so that temperature of mixture remains at 130° to 140°F for 4 to 5 hours (use a warm stove, top of refrigerator, or put bowl in a pan of hot water).

4. Taste not sweet enough? Cover and let mix "culture" another 3 hours.

5. Wrap rice-sprout mixture in cheesecloth and squeeze so that any liquid passes through cheesecloth and returns to saucepan. (Keep leftover grain to make rice pudding.) Bring liquid to a boil. Using candy thermometer, cook until liquid becomes suitably syrupy and thermometer registers 140°F.

Options: 1. Use as a pancake syrup or dessert sauce. 2. To make your own sprouts, see recipe for Wheat Sprout Sugar, p. 00.

Makes 3 cups syrup; 25 calories each tablespoon

Did you know that if anything from the hive gives you hives, you can safely break out the rice? Brown rice is one of the least allergy-provoking of all grains, is rich in B vitamins, and is more easily assimilated by your digestive system without causing unpleasant seesawing of blood sugar levels. White rice is super refined like white sugar. Skip it.

Breads and Cereals

Breads

No milk
No corn
No refined sugar

No wheat (optional)
No eggs (optional)
No yeast
No citrus

Milk-free Muffins (Tofu-Oat Bread)

1 cup pastry flour
1 cup quick-cooking oats
1 teaspoon corn-free baking powder
2 teaspoons baking soda
1 teaspoon cinnamon
2 eggs, separated
8 ounces tofu
¼ cup vegetable or nut oil
1/3 cup honey
1 teaspoon vanilla

1. Preheat oven to 425°F.

2. In a bowl, combine flour, oats, baking powder, baking soda, and cinnamon.

3. Put yolks in a blender with tofu, oil, honey, and vanilla. Blend well then mix with dry ingredients.

4. Beat whites until stiff and fold into batter.

5. Spoon into 12 lightly greased muffin cups and bake for 15 minutes (or until lightly browned).

Options: 1. Can't have wheat? Eliminate flour and substitute an extra cup of oats, finely ground in blender until powdery. Increase baking powder to 3 teaspoons. 2. Can't have eggs? Omit, and increase tofu to 16 ounces. 3. A pinch of the vanilla-flavored herb dried woodruff can be used instead of vanilla.

Makes 8–10 muffins; 110 calories each

Did you know that when it's dessert time, as a nation we eat 700 million Twinkies and individually we eat 9 pounds of bananas and 33 quarts of popcorn annually?

No refined sugar
No soy
No wheat
No corn
No yeast
No chocolate

Brownie Bagels

½ cup any dry homemade sugar (see p. 79)
3 teaspoons baking powder
1 cup potato-starch flour
3 cups ground rolled oats
1/3 cup carob powder
2/3 cup vegetable or nut oil
2 eggs, beaten
2 tablespoons any cream substitute (see p. 74)
1 tablespoon melted butter or vegetable or nut oil

1. In a large mixing bowl combine homemade sugar, baking powder, flour, oats, and carob. Make hole in center of dry ingredients and add nearly all of oil (retaining a little), eggs, cream substitute, and vanilla. Stir until ingredients are moistened.

2. Turn onto lightly floured board and roll dough ½ inch thick. Cut with a 2¼-inch floured doughnut cutter. Place "bagels" on greased baking sheet, 1 inch apart. Cover, refrigerate for 1½ hours or overnight.

3. Preheat oven to 400°F. Brush bagels with melted butter or oil. Bake 10 minutes.

Options: 1. Bake as doughnuts in a doughnut machine instead of oven. 2. Or make Brownie Waffles—reduce oats to 2½ cups, increase sugar by 2 tablespoons. Bake on hot greased waffle iron.

Makes 2 dozen; about 100 calories per bagel, 75 per waffle

No wheat
No refined sugar
No nuts
No soy

Spice Krispies

Serve with sliced fruit and milk or milk substitute. Also good as a snack.

2 tablespoons melted, unsalted butter
4 cups unseasoned popcorn
*   spices*

1. Preheat oven to 400°F.

2. In a baking pan, drizzle melted butter over popcorn. Sprinkle with spices. Mix well.

3. Bake for 5 minutes.

Options: 1. Make Frosted Spice Krispies—heat ¼ cup honey to a boil, reduce to a simmer, and heat for 8 minutes. Add to popped corn. Toss to coat kernels. Spread on cookie sheet. Bake until brown. Watch carefully, stirring once. Use corn oil or corn germ oil instead of butter. 3. Omit spice. Substitute any Dessert Sprinkle (see p. 83).

Makes 4 1-cup servings; 65 calories per cup plain without milk, 100 per cup frosted

Did you know the spice you pick can make your cereal an upper or a downer? According to Dr. George Schwartz in his book *Food Power,* cinnamon and nutmeg, along with ginger and mace, are classified as stimulants, while allspice, anise, and cardamom are considered tranquilizers.

No soy
No nuts
No refined sugar
No citrus
No spices

Mock Grape-Nuts

Serve with cream and honey or a dry sugar substitute.

1½ cups rolled oats
1 cup brown rice flour (see Note)
1½ cups cornmeal
1½ cups whole-wheat flour
2 tablespoons date sugar
2 cups skim milk or Dessert Milk

1. Preheat over to 325°F.

2. In a bowl mix dry ingredients, add enough milk to make a stiff dough.

3. Roll out into a very thin sheet, cut into strips, and bake until light brown. Cool.

4. Put through a food grinder on coarse blade. Should be gritty.

Note: To make your own brown rice flour, toast brown rice for 20 minutes at 325°F, grind in a grain mill, processor, or heavy-duty blender until powdered. Store in cool pantry.

Options: 1. Use milk substitute in place of whole milk. 2. Use homemade grain sugar (see Homemade Sugars, Sweeteners, and Syrups) in place of date sugar.

Makes 6 6-ounce servings, about 100 calories each, without milk or sweetening

Did you know that if you wash dishes you burn 67 calories and if you go for a half-mile walk you'll burn twice as many? If you do both, you can have a second helping of Mock Grape-Nuts and still be in the caloric black.

No nuts
No wheat
No refined sugar
No corn

No-Nut Granola

2 cups rolled oats
1 cup rye flakes (see Note)
Cinnamon to taste
Pinch dried lemon peel
¼ cup date sugar or maple syrup granules

1. Preheat oven to 325°F.

2. Place oats and rye flakes in a colander. Pour water over them to dampen. Drain well and spread in a thin layer in a shallow baking pan or on cookie sheet.

3. Place in oven. Toast, stirring from time to time to avoid overbrowning, 20 to 30 minutes.

4. Sprinkle lightly with cinnamon and lemon peel and sift in sweetener.

5. Cool and store covered in dry place.

Options: 1. Any flaked grain may be used in place of rye (wheat, barley, rice, etc.—available at health food stores) or simply omit and increase oats to 3 cups. 2. Heat and use as a substitute for dry roasted peanuts. Use cold as a brownbag snack. Or sprinkle over hot cereal to add crunch. 3. Allergic to cinnamon and/or lemon? Try ½ teaspoon coriander. It's a good substitute for both.

Makes three 1-cup servings; 100 calories per serving

Did you know that the antioxidant chemicals BHA and BHT are added to numerous commercial granolas and dry cereals (as well as candies and baked goods) have caused serious growth retardation in test animals? It is also a major cause of allergic reactions in humans, says the *Dictionary of Health and Nutrition.*

No wheat
No eggs

No milk
No soy
No refined sugar
No nuts
No yeast
No wheat

Apple Crisp

The granola alternative. Use as a cereal, snack, or dessert.

¼ cup Rice Syrup (see p. 90) or light molasses
2 tablespoons apple juice
½ teaspoon vanilla
4 cups popcorn
2 apples, cored, peeled, and cut into bite-size chunks
¼ cup water
¼ teaspoon cinnamon
¼ cup raisins (optional)

1. Place sweetener and apple juice in a small saucepan over high heat. Bring to boil, stirring constantly.

2. Reduce heat to low, and simmer for 8 minutes. Remove from heat, stir in vanilla, and pour mixture over popcorn in a bowl. Use 2 forks to toss well.

3. Place apple chunks and water in a small saucepan. Cover and steam over medium heat, just until softened (about 5 minutes).

4. Dust cinnamon over apples; add raisins. Cover and cook over very low heat for 1 minute to steam raisins (if used).

5. Spoon popcorn mixture into 4 bowls. Spoon apple-raisin mixture over each.

Options: 1. Substitute another juice and another fruit, such as pineapple juice and pineapple chunks. 2. Use maple syrup or honey in place of syrup or molasses. 3. Use ¼ cup any spicy tea in place of water and cinnamon.

Makes 4 servings; about 85 calories each

Did you know that 1 cup of pineapple juice supplies 200 units of infection-fighting vitamin A?

Cookies, Cakes, and Frostings

Cookies

No chocolate
No eggs
No milk
No soy
No refined sugar
No yeast

Unbaked Christmas Cookies

3 cups ground sprouted wheat berries
1 cup chopped walnuts
½ cup sesame seed
1 cup raisins, soaked in boiling water until plump
2 ripe bananas, mashed
1 tablespoon blackstrap molasses
12–16 soft pitted dates, chopped
1 teaspoon cinnamon
⅛ teaspoon cloves
Pinch ground aniseed (optional)
1½ cups shredded coconut

In a mixing bowl combine all ingredients except coconut. Roll into balls, then roll balls in coconut, and refrigerate.

Options: 1. Cooked version: Roll into balls. Roll balls in coconut, flatten them on greased cookie sheet, and bake 15 minutes at 350°F. 2. Substitute any other sprouted nut or grain for wheat. 3. Omit sprouts. Substitute ¼ teaspoon dried mint or chamomile tea leaves.

Makes 4 dozen cookies; about 80 calories each

Did you know that dried dates have a higher sugar content than any other common fruit, are twice as sweet as fresh dates, and provide five times as much calcium as bananas?

No soy
No chocolate
No refined sugar
No wheat
No corn
No citrus
No yeast

Brownstones (Imitation Peanut Butter Cookies)

6 tablespoons tahini (sesame seed butter)
2 tablespoons honey
½ cup chopped walnuts
½ cup pitted dates, soaked in boiling water until soft and drained
½ teaspoon cinnamon
1½ cups rolled oats

1. Preheat oven to 350°F.

2. Stir tahini and honey together. Add nuts.

3. Puree softened dates in blender and add to mixture.

4. Add cinnamon mixed with oats. Stir until blended.

5. Drop by teaspoonfuls on buttered or foil-covered cookie sheet. Bake for about 10 to 15 minutes or until edges are brown.

Options: 1. Use honey in place of pureed dates. 2. Try crushed cassia buds (available at all health food stores) in place of cinnamon. 3. Use triticale or rye flakes instead of oats.

Makes 2½ dozen cookies; 50 calories each cookie

Did you know that in ancient Greece the walnut was considered a fertility symbol and was used to treat mental illness?

No refined sugar
No milk
No wheat
No soy
No yeast
No corn
No spices

Maroon Macaroons

2 egg whites
1/3 cup Apple Fructose (see p. 86)
1 cup rolled oats
½ cup grated coconut

1. Preheat oven to 350°F.

2. Beat whites in a small bowl until stiff.

3. Combine fructose and oats in another bowl. Mix until well combined.

4. Add coconut. Fold in beaten whites.

5. Drop by spoonfuls onto parchment or foil-lined cookie sheet. Bake for 12 minutes.

Makes 20 to 24 macaroons; 35 calories each

Did you know that when it's hot and humid, you can serve home-baked cookies straight from the freezer without thawing? They're cool and supercrisp this way.

No refined sugar
No milk
No wheat
No corn
No spices
No citrus
No eggs
No yeast

Unbutter Cookies

1 cup apple juice
1 cup dried dates
2/3 cup nut or vegetable oil
1 large apple, cored, peeled, and grated
3 cups rolled oats plus 1 cup arrowroot powder
1 cup chopped nuts (of those allowed)

1. Preheat oven to 350°F.

2. In a saucepan, pour ½ cup apple juice over dates, and cook until they are soft. Puree in a blender to make a paste. Add oil.

3. Stir in apple. Add oats and arrowroot, nuts, and remaining juice. Let dough rest 10 minutes.

4. Drop by spoonfuls onto lightly greased cookie sheets, flatten dough. Bake for 15 minutes.

Options: 1. Use 1 cup mixed dried fruit in place of dates. 2. Use 1 cup chopped sprouts in place of nuts. 3. Substitute 1 cup chamomile tea for juice (it's a better-than-apple-juice analog). 4. Use 2/3 cup dried dates and 1/3 cup date sugar in place of second ingredient.

Makes 2 dozen big cookies or 4 dozen small ones.

Did you know that 1 tablespoon honey contains no fiber and 60 calories, while 1 tablespoon of granulated dried dates has 40 calories and almost .58 gram of bowel-regulating fruit fiber?

No refined sugar
No wheat
No eggs
No soy
No corn
No yeast
No citrus

Saucepan Cookies (No-Bake Oatmeal Crisps)

2/3 cup maple syrup
¼ cup any permitted nut or vegetable oil
5 tablespoons carob powder
1 teaspoon cinnamon
½ cup peanut butter
1 cup rolled oats
1 teaspoon vanilla

1. Put syrup, oil, carob, and cinnamon in a saucepan, and blend well.

2. Boil for 3 minutes, stirring constantly. Remove from heat and stir in remaining ingredients.

3. Drop on cookie sheet by spoonfuls and cover with wax paper. Cool and remove from sheet.

Options: 1. Substitute tahini or almond butter for peanut butter. 2. Try ground coriander instead of cinnamon. 3. Use Apple Fructose (see p. 86) in place of maple syrup for reduced sweetness and fewer calories. 4. Substitute ¼ cup chopped sprouted fenugreek for oats.

Makes 2 dozen cookies; 25 calories each cookie

Did you know that the fenugreek seed is one of the ten fastest seeds of all to sprout? It's ready to eat two days after germination and it has a flavor similar to maple syrup.

No wheat
No corn
No refined sugar
No citrus
No milk
No yeast
No spices

Hypoallergenic Nut Jumbles

2 cups shelled filberts or walnuts (or other nuts)
1 large egg
½–¾ cup maple syrup
½ cup pecan pieces

1. Preheat oven to 325°F.

2. Grind the mixed nuts to a powder in a blender or food processor.

3. Mix well with the egg, maple syrup, and pecans.

4. Spoon batter by teaspoonfuls onto an oiled baking sheet.

5. Bake for about 45 minutes, until dry and firm.

Note: Cookies will stay chewy but won't remain hard as long as cookies that are made with wheat. Eat within a week.

Options: 1. Use honey, Rice Syrup (p. 90) or Apple Fructose (p. 86) in place of maple syrup. 2. Can't tolerate walnuts, filberts, or pecans? Try cashews, peanuts, and/or sunflower seed. 3. Add ½ teaspoon grated lemon or orange peel.

Makes about 1½ dozen cookies; 100 calories each

Did you know that filberts (also known as hazelnuts) contain ten times as much protein as bananas, are easily digested, and have half the cholesterol-regulating fiber of raisins?

No wheat
No refined sugar
No corn
No soy
No baking yeast
No citrus
No spices

Shortcut Shortcake

Using a waffle iron to "bake" this shortcake saves heating oven and yields a rich, crisp dessert in a hurry.

1 cup barley flour
1 teaspoon maple syrup granules or any homemade dry sugar
2 teaspoons corn-free baking powder
2 tablespoons vegetable oil
½ cup whole milk
1 egg, beaten

1. Mix and sift the dry ingredients in a bowl.

2. Combine oil, milk, and egg; add to the dry ingredients and mix lightly. (Dough should be soft, but thick enough to hold its shape.)

3. Spoon 1 tablespoon into hot waffle iron and cook until lightly browned. Repeat until batter is used up.

4. Top with Spirited Fruits (p. 137), or stewed fruit plus any milk-free whipped topping (see Toppings and Dessert Sauces).

Options: 1. Any mixture of oat, barley, and rice flours can be substituted for barley; all are available at health food stores. 2. Substitute ½ cup pureed tofu for milk.

Makes 8 shortcakes; 50 calories each

Did you know that barley provides many of wheat's nutrients without its allergenic properties? The world's oldest cultivated grain, barley is rich in B vitamins and the minerals potassium, phosphorus, and sulfur.

No refined sugar
No sugar
No eggs
No milk
No baking yeast
No corn
No soy
No spices

Sweet Wheat Cake

Makes a cake that's in the moist applesauce cake tradition, yet free of the traditional allergens that cake contains.

1 gallon sprouted wheat (see Note)
3 apples, cored, peeled, and grated
Sesame seed

1. Preheat oven to 350°F.

2. Grind the sprouted wheat into a dough in a grinder or food

processor (it may be necessary to grind the sprouts twice to get a dough of good consistency).

3. Add remaining ingredients, and form into a ball. Place on lightly greased glass 8-inch pie plate sprinkled with sesame seed.

4. Bake for 1½ hours or until done at center. Test with a toothpick or skewer; if it comes out clean it is finished.

Options: 1. Substitute another sprouted grain for the wheat sprouts. 2. Substitute coriander for cinnamon. 3. Use grated pears or carrots in place of apples. 4. Make Sweet Wheat Bread Sticks instead. After forming dough, shape into long rolls. Twirl in sesame or poppy seed and bake 30 minutes.

Makes 8 to 10 servings; about 75 calories each

Note: Wheat already sprouted is sold by many health food stores and natural food restaurants. Or do it yourself.

No wheat
No refined sugar
No yeast
No milk (optional)
No spices

Upside Downside Cake

¼ *cup butter*
2 *cups cored, peeled, and sliced apples*
1 *egg*
½ *cup chopped almonds*
½ *cup maple syrup granules or homemade dry sugar*
1½ *cups ground rolled oats*
2 *teaspoons baking powder*
Grated rind of 1 orange (optional)
½ *cup whole milk or milk substitute*

1. Preheat oven to 325°F.

2. In a 9-inch oven-proof skillet, melt butter. Add apples and nuts. Sauté.

3. Set aside. Beat egg, adding "sugar" gradually. Combine egg–sugar mixture with dry ingredients, and orange rind. Add milk and mix thoroughly.

4. Pour batter over apples in skillet. Bake for 35 minutes or until cake is firm. Loosen edges and invert cake on serving plate. Eat either side up. Serve with thick cream or frosting (see recipes in this section).

Options: 1. Use plums, peaches, or apricots in place of apples. 2. Dairy-free version—substitute any nut butter (peanut, almond, cashew, etc., available at health food stores) for butter. Use any milk substitute for milk. 3. Use any wheat flour substitute in place of oats.

Makes a 9-inch cake or 1 dozen cupcakes; 95 calories each serving

No chocolate
No corn
No milk
No yeast
No refined sugar
No spices

Boston Baked Brownies

½ cup dry roasted soybeans
½ cup butter or permitted nut or vegetable oil
2/3 cup honey
2 eggs
1 teaspoon almond extract
1 teaspoon powdered kelp
½ cup carob powder
2/3 cup unbleached or whole-wheat pastry flour
1 teaspoon corn-free baking powder

1. Preheat oven to 350°.

2. Crush beans to a cornmeal consistency in a blender, food processor, or with a rolling pin.

3. In a bowl cream butter and honey. Beat in eggs one at a time. Add extract.

4. Sift together dry ingredients and stir into batter. Turn into 9-inch square pan.

5. Bake 30 minutes. Let cool and cut into squares.

Options: 1. Substitute Spicy Honey Syrup (see recipe p. 89) for honey. 2. Use walnuts in place of beans. 3. Substitute 1 cup of pureed tofu for eggs and increase baking powder to 2 teaspoons.

Makes 18 squares; 75 calories each

Did you know that kelp, which can be used as a salt or a pepper substitute, contains eleven times more calcium than spinach? And calcium can help counteract allergic reactions to pollution? A dose of 500 milligrams three times a day helps.

No wheat
No eggs
No milk
No soy
No citrus
No refined sugar
No yeast

Crumb Buns

½ cup raisins
½ cup chopped dried peaches or apricots
1 cup chopped sun-dried pineapple
½ teaspoon ground ginger
1 cup water plus 2 tablespoons
1 cup rolled oats
1 cup whole-wheat flour substitute (see chapter II)
¼ cup any permitted nut or vegetable oil

1. Preheat oven to 350°F.

2. Combine the first four ingredients plus 1 cup water in a quart saucepan.

3. Simmer, covered, for 5 minutes or until fruit is tender.

4. Combine remaining ingredients in a bowl. Press two-thirds of the oat mixture into bottom of an ungreased 8"x8"x2" baking pan.

5. Spread fruit over this. Then crumble remainder of oats over the fruit. Bake for 30 to 35 minutes. Cool before cutting. Serve warm or cold.

Options: 1. Use ½ teaspoon powdered cloves in place of ginger. 2. Substitute chopped drained pineapple in place of dried pineapple. Or use 2 cups chopped unsulfured mixed dried fruits in place of first three ingredients.

Makes 12 crumbly servings; about 150 calories each

Did you know that manganese can help stop a sugar craving? The dessert spice highest in this trace mineral is cloves, with 263 ppm (parts per million). Cloves also contain 80.9 milligrams of vitamin C—twice as much as allspice or cinnamon.

No wheat
No refined sugar
No corn
No spices
No soy
No baking yeast

Barley Birthday Cake

1 cup barley flour (see Options)
3 teaspoons low-sodium baking powder
4 tablespoons nut or vegetable oil
½ cup dry homemade sugar
2/3 cup whole milk or milk substitute
1 egg
½ teaspoon vanilla

1. Preheat oven to 375°F.

2. Sift flour and baking powder together in a bowl. Set aside.

3. Add "sugar" to oil. Beat until blended and set aside.

4. In another bowl, beat milk or milk substitute, egg, and vanilla. Add oil and "sugar" mixture. Then add sifted dry ingredients.

5. Bake in two greased 6-inch pans for about 40 minutes.

6. When cool, frost both layers. Use Fast Pastel Frosting (p. 113) or 5-Minute Maple Dribble (p. 89).

Options: 1. Omit egg. Use a substitute (see chapter II, p. 50). 2. Substitute rice flour for barley flour, both of which are available at health food stores. 3. To bake as cupcakes reduce oven time to 25 minutes.

Makes 10 to 12 servings; about 75 calories each

Did you know that the nutritional supplement L-glutamine can help control an allergic craving for sugar? L-glutamine is the amide form of glutamic acid (an amino acid). In the brain, L-glutamine is broken down to form a fuel for the brain, says Dr. Abram Hoffer. It is also tasteless and completely nontoxic; 1 to 2 grams does the job.

No wheat
No milk
No spices
No corn
No refined sugar
No yeast

Cherry Sponge Cake

4 egg yolks
½ cup brown rice flour plus 2 tablespoons soy flour
1 teaspoon baking powder
1 teaspoon vanilla
1 teaspoon almond extract
4 egg whites, beaten
1/3 cup Liquid Cherries

1. Preheat oven to 325°F.

2. Beat the egg yolks until thick and lemony in a bowl. Sift the rice and soy flours with baking powder and combine with egg yolks.

3. Add vanilla and almond extracts. Beat egg whites until stiff. Then beat in Liquid Cherries very slowly, beating to a thick meringue.

4. Fold in the rice flour–egg yolk mixture. Bake in two 6-inch pans, a square pan, or a tube pan, for 25 minutes.

5. Cake will fall a bit as it cools.

Options: 1. Substitute Apple Fructose (p. 86) or honey for Liquid Cherries. 2. Substitute ½ teaspoon cherry concentrate (see Appendix B, Mail Order Sources) for vanilla. 3. Substitute potato flour (high in vitamin C) for rice flour (high in vitamin B).

Makes 10 slices; 75 calories each serving

Did you know that if you replace 2 tablespoons wheat flour with 2 tablespoons soy flour for every cup of flour used, this greatly enhances the protein value of your baked goods? This is because wheat (a grain) and soy (a bean) contain complementary protein.

No soy
No refined sugar
No corn
No milk
No yeast
No citrus

Pinto Bean Fruit Cake

2 cups well-cooked pinto beans
¼ cup cooking liquid from beans
½ cup butter
1 cup Wheat Sugar (see p. 80)
2 teaspoons vanilla
1 egg
1 cup pastry flour
1 teaspoon baking soda
1 teaspoon cinnamon
½ teaspoon ground cloves
½ teaspoon allspice
½ teaspoon mace
2 cups cored, peeled, and finely chopped apples
1 cup seedless raisins
½ cup chopped walnuts or pecans

1. Preheat oven to 350°F.

2. In a bowl mash beans with bean liquid, using potato masher or electric mixer.

3. In another bowl cream butter, adding "sugar" gradually, and beat until fluffy. Add vanilla and egg. Beat well, then beat in mashed beans. Mix thoroughly.

4. Sift together flour, baking soda, and spices. Add half to the batter and stir until just mixed.

5. Add apples, raisins, nuts, and remaining flour. Stir until just mixed.

6. Spoon into buttered 9-inch tube cake pan. Bake for 1 hour. Cool.

Options: 1. Replace pinto beans with soybeans or other tolerated legumes. 2. Use any allowed oil in place of butter and replace Wheat Sugar with Plain Grain Sugar. 3. Omit nuts and substitute chopped alfalfa or wheat sprouts.

Makes 24 slices; about 150 calories each

Did you know that pinto beans, which are a source of fat-free proteins, amino acids, B vitamins, and minerals, lose their spots when cooked?

No chocolate
No refined sugar
No wheat
No corn
No spices
No nuts

Three Fast Frostings

Fast Fudge:
6 ounces unsweetened carob chips
6 teaspoons butter

Melt carob chips with butter over low heat, stirring constantly. Spread over 6 large cupcakes or spoon over frozen desserts.

Option: Add ¼ teaspoon vanilla.

Fast Pastel:
½ cup sugar-free fruit jelly
1 egg
2 tablespoons lemon juice
½ cup melted butter
Sifted milk powder or arrowroot powder

Combine jelly, egg, lemon juice, melted butter, and enough sifted milk powder or arrowroot powder to produce spreading consistency. Whip smooth in blender. Ices 1 two-layer cake.

Option: Omit egg. Use a substitute (see chapter II).

Fast Crunchy:
4 tablespoons honey
1/3 cup oats-only, crushed granola or ready-to-eat dry cereal

Heat honey in a small saucepan, and stir in crushed oats-only granola or dry cereal. Spread on cake or cupcakes while warm. Frosts 6 cupcakes.

Option: Use maple syrup, omit honey.

Pies and Piecrusts

Pies

No refined sugar
No milk
No wheat
No corn
No eggs
No spices
No nuts

Humble Pie

5 medium apples, cored and peeled
1½ cups water, or 1 cup Simple Honey Syrup (see p. 88) and ½
    cup water
½ cup chopped pitted dates
1 tablespoon agar or plain gelatin
1 8-inch piecrust

1. Chop apples or slice. Place in saucepan with water or syrup mixture and cook until soft.

2. Pour into a blender or processor with dates and gelatin or agar.

3. Process (using chopping button on blender), but just blend enough so that apple mixture is still a bit chunky.

4. Pour into a piecrust of your choice. Chill.

Options: 1. For a not-as-sweet variation, substitute cooked acorn squash. 2. Garnish with sliced kiwi-fruit or fresh kumquats. 3. Omit crust and pour filling into a greased casserole or cake pan. Serve as a pudding.

Makes 12 servings; 125 calories each

Did you know that there are at least 108 kinds of pies on record, including mock cherry, green currant, yellow raspberry, Dutch blackberry, buttermilk, quince, Roosevelt, chocolate, humbug, and popcorn?

No refined sugar
No soy
No wheat
No eggs
No corn
No milk
No spices

Counterfeit Key Lime Pie

3 small (10 ounces each) thick-skinned avocados
¾ cup lime juice
½ cup honey
3 tablespoons loosely packed coriander leaves, or ½ teaspoon
  ground coriander
Lime slices

1. Cut avocados in half. Scoop out avocado and save shells. Rinse and dry shells and set aside.

2. Whirl enough avocado in blender to make 3 cups.

3. Then add lime juice, honey, and coriander to blender.

4. Blend until smooth. Pour into a shallow glass dish. Cover and freeze.

5. Remove from freezer. Spoon scoops of the soft ice into shells. Refreeze.

6. Garnish each with a thin slice of lime when ready to serve.

Options: 1. Citrus a forbidden fruit? Then substitute pineapple juice. 2. Spoon filling into any prebaked tarts or piecrusts (see Piecrusts) instead of avocado shells. 3. Use Simple Honey Syrup in place of honey to lower calories.

Makes about 4 cups or 6 servings of 2/3 cup each; 100 calories each cup

Did you know Americans buy 400 million pounds of frozen baked pies each year, twice the combined volume of other frozen baked goods?

No eggs
No milk
No wheat
No refined sugar
No corn

Health Mincemeat

4 tart-flavored apples, cored, peeled, and chopped
½ cup apple juice
1½ cups raisins
Grated rind of 1 orange
½ cup orange juice
2 cups walnuts or mixed raw nuts
¼ teaspoon cinnamon
¼–½ teaspoon cloves, allspice, or coriander
2 tablespoons sweet miso sweetener
1 9-inch piecrust

1. Combine first 5 ingredients in a heavy pot. Bring to a boil, and simmer for 30 minutes.

2. Add next 3 ingredients and the miso or Paste, creamed, in a little of the cooking liquid. Mix well, remove from heat, and allow to cool to room temperature.

3. Pour into piecrust and serve.

Options: 1. Replace spices with ½ teaspoon powdered rose-hips herbs or ½ teaspoon almond extract. 2. Use papaya juice in place of orange juice. 3. Replace apple juice with cranberry juice.

Makes 10 servings; 110 calories each without crust

Did you know you can prevent custard-type pies from becoming soggy? Coat the uncooked shell with a little egg white. Tilt the pie around (or use pastry brush) until the egg white has rolled across all surfaces. Pour excess off immediately. Bake coated shell 1 minute. It should look shiny. To avoid spills, pour filling into pie shell as it sits on oven rack. Bake at 350°F for about an hour or until custard is set. (To bake un-coated, unfilled shell, set oven at 425°F for 8 to 12 minutes.)

No chocolate
No refined sugar
No eggs
No spices
No nuts

Brownie Pie

4 ounces sugar-free block carob or carob chips
⅓ cup whole milk
2 tablespoons any homemade dry sugar (see p. 79)
3 ounces low-fat cream cheese, softened
8 ounces whipped topping (see Note)
1 prebaked 8-inch piecrust

1. Heat carob and 2 tablespoons of the milk in a saucepan over low heat, stirring until carob is melted.

2. In a bowl beat "sugar" into cream cheese. Add remaining milk and carob mixture and beat until smooth.

3. Fold carob mixture into whipped topping. Blend until smooth.

4. Spoon into prebaked pie shell and freeze until firm, about 4 hours.

Note: Puree 1 cup plain tofu with 1 tablespoon honey and 1 teaspoon vanilla extract in blender to make whipped topping.

Options: 1. Use any homemade milk substitute in place of dairy milk (see Milk and Cream Substitutes). 2. Substitute 3 ounces ricotta cheese for cream cheese. It's sweeter than cottage cheese, and only 10 percent more calories. 3. Omit crust. Chill and serve as a pudding.

Makes one 8-inch pie; 75 calories per slice

Did you know a second way to prevent soggy pie bottoms in a custard pie is to bake custard filling by itself in a pie plate and bake the pie shell separately? Then cut pie in wedges and place in shell. Hide the cuts by "frosting" top with whipped topping.

Piecrusts

No corn
No soy
No wheat
No flour
No refined sugar
No eggs (optional)
No spices
No yeast

Quick Wheat-Free Piecrust

4 cups cooked barley
1 cup shredded coconut
3 eggs, beaten
3 tablespoons melted butter

1. Preheat oven to 350°F.

2. Combine all ingredients in a bowl.

3. Press into two 8-inch pie pans.

4. Bake 10 to 12 minutes or until brown.

Options: 1. Use cooked rice, cooked buckwheat, or cooked millet in place of barley. 2. Substitute 1 cup Dessert Sprinkles (see p. 83) for coconut. 3. In place of eggs use 2 tablespoons agar plus 2 tablespoons flaxseed simmered in 1 cup water for 5 minutes.

Makes two 8-inch piecrusts; 50 calories per wedge

Did you know that the cheesecake, which is really a pie, contains seven to ten allergens and that Sara Lee makes 90,000 cheesecakes a day?

No soy
No wheat
No corn
No refined sugar
No spices
No milk
No yeast

Rice Cake Piecrust

5 unsalted rice cakes (see Options)
4 egg whites

1. Preheat oven to 350°F.

2. Break rice cakes into chunks, crush in blender to a fine powder. In a bowl whip egg whites with a beater or wire whip until they form stiff peaks.

3. Pour rice cake "powder" onto egg whites. Mix well to form a dough that is spongy to the touch.

4. Spoon into an 8-inch pie plate, patting the dough flat with a spatula or back of a spoon. Dough may appear grainy and rough, but after baking it will have a meringuelike texture.

5. Bake for 12 minutes. Remove from oven and let cool thoroughly before adding filling.

Options: 1. Use 2½ to 3 cups salt-free puffed rice in place of rice cakes, sold at health food stores. 2. Add ¼ teaspoon nutmeg or allspice. 3. Substitute unsalted puffed wheat or corn for rice.

Makes one 8-inch pie shell

Did you know that Pennsylvania Dutch shoofly pie isn't really a pie but traditionally a dessert made when there was nothing else to fill a pie shell? The pie is simply a mixture of molasses, water, baking soda, and salt poured into an unbaked pie shell and sprinkled with a crumb topping, then baked.

No refined sugar
No chocolate
No wheat
No yeast
No spices
No milk
No citrus

2-Ingredient Apple Piecrust

5 dozen dried apples, cut into pieces
1 tablespoon carob powder

1. Grind apples on coarse blade in a food grinder or use food processor.

2. Use a wet fork to press into a 9-inch pie pan. Sprinkle with carob.

3. Freeze crust while preparing any filling (use any ready-to-eat fruit dessert or pudding, sherbet, or cooked grain dessert).

4. Just before serving run paring knife around the edge of crust to loosen and facilitate cutting and serving. Top with milk-free Whipped Topping (see p. 150).

Options: 1. Substitute 50 dates or 50 figs for apples. 2. Substitute 1 tablespoon whey powder or arrowroot for carob. 3. Chill crust and cut into squares. Eat as fruit fudge rather than piecrust.

Makes one 9-inch pie shell

No corn
No wheat
No milk
No eggs
No spices
No butter
No refined sugar
No soy

2-Ingredient Rice Piecrust

2 cups raw long-grain brown rice
3 cups water

1. Place rice in a sieve and rinse under cold running water.

2. Place rice in large (10- or 12-inch), heavy skillet. Add the water. Bring to boil and cook, uncovered, about 10 minutes until most of liquid evaporates. Cover tightly and cook over very low heat 20 to 25 minutes.

3. Scoop out most of the soft rice from the center but leave a border of rice about ½ inch thick in the skillet. Leave a bottom shell of rice about ½ inch deep (serve the scooped-out rice later in soup, etc.).

4. Return rice crust to heat and cook over low flame (using an asbestos pad) for 1 hour—or until rice pulls away from sides and can be removed easily. Shell should be well dried and have a crusty brown appearance. You should now be able to turn out pie shell in one piece.

Options: 1. Break shell into crackers and eat as a low-calorie, high-fiber snack. 2. Substitute 1 cup cracked rye or cracked buckwheat (groats or kasha) for 1 cup rice for a combination crust.

Makes one large 10-inch or 12-inch pie shell

No refined sugar
No wheat
No corn
No milk
No spices

Three More 2-Ingredient Piecrusts

All three piecrusts may be cooled, frozen, and filled another day.

Apple-Oat:

2 cups quick-cooling rolled oats
1 cup unsweetened applesauce (any fruit may be substituted)

1. Preheat oven to 350°F.

2. Mix ingredients and press into two 8-inch pie tins.

3. Bake for 25 minutes. Cool and fill.

Makes two 8-inch pie shells

Sesame-Oat:

2/3 cup ground rolled oats
1/3 cup ground sesame seed

1. Preheat oven to 350°F.

2. Combine ingredients in a bowl.

3. Add enough water to form the dough. Press into an 8-inch pie pan.

4. Bake for 20 minutes. Cool and fill.

Makes one 8-inch pie shell

Coconut-Peanut:

1 cup coconut
2 tablespoons peanut oil (vegetable oil may be substituted)

1. Preheat oven to 350°F.

2. Mix coconut and oil. Press into an 8-inch pie pan.

3. Bake until edges brown. Cool and fill.

Makes one 8-inch pie shell

Puddings and Other Whipped Desserts

Puddings

No eggs
No milk
No refined sugar
No nuts
No spices
No corn
No soy

Eggless Rice Pudding

1 cup water
2 tablespoons agar plus 2 tablespoons flaxseed (replaces eggs)
2 cups cooked rice
¼–½ cup honey
1 teaspoon vanilla
Nutmeg, cinnamon, and powdered ginger to taste

1. Combine water and agar-flaxseed mixture together in saucepan and simmer 5 minutes. Remove from heat.

2. Mix with rest of ingredients in a bowl.

3. Refrigerate an hour or so before serving.

Options: 1. Use 2 cups cooked millet, wheat kernels, or whole rye berries (all available at health food stores) in place of rice. 2. Use maple syrup or Apple Fructose (see p. 86) in place of honey.

Makes 4 servings; 100 calories each

Did you know that cinnamon is number eight on America's best-loved spices list? And that nutmeg barely makes the hit parade? (Pepper is number one.)

No milk
No eggs
No citrus
No refined sugar
No wheat

Sugar-free Pudding on a Stick

3 cakes tofu
1½ teaspoons vanilla
2 tablespoons lemon juice
1 10-ounce package frozen raspberries, thawed and drained
1 ripe banana, mashed
½ cup honey

1. Blend ingredients in a bowl by hand or with an electric mixer.

2. Freeze in paper cups or Popsicle molds. Insert wooden sucker sticks when half frozen.

Options: 1. Substitute a 10-ounce package of frozen strawberries for raspberries. 2. Use Apple Fructose (see p. 86) in place of honey.

Makes 8 to 10 "pops"; 75 calories each

Did you know you can rejuvenate tofu that's more than ten days old? Yes, old tofu can be refreshed by parboiling. Bring 1 quart water to a boil, reduce heat to low, drop in tofu. Cover and heat for 2 to 3 minutes. Remove tofu, drain, and use. To keep it even longer, drain and freeze. When defrosted, it will be more porous, chewy, and versatile.

No refined sugar
No citrus
No corn
No eggs
No milk
No citrus

Sour Grapes (Semisweet Fruit Pudding)

2 cups unsweetened grape juice
1 tablespoon Fruit Fructose Paste (see p. 85)
3 tablespoons arrowroot powder
1 drop oil of cinnamon (see Options)
⅛ teaspoon ground cloves
¼ teaspoon anise extract
4 orange slices
4 teaspoons chopped walnuts

1. In a heavy saucepan, bring 1½ cups grape juice and fructose to a boil.

2. Mix remaining juice with arrowroot in a small bowl and slowly add it to boiling juice, stirring constantly.

3. Add cinnamon oil and cloves and cook until thickened.

4. When thickened, stir in anise extract; remove from heat.

5. Pour into wineglasses and chill. Garnish each with an orange slice and 1 teaspoon chopped walnuts.

Options: 1. For sweeter version, use 2 tablespoons fructose or 2 tablespoons thick honey. 2. Use powdered cinnamon in place of oil of cinnamon (available at health food stores) and fennel seed instead of anise extract for an anise flavor plus crunch.

Makes 4 servings; 120 calories each

Did you know oil of cinnamon is said to be a sure cure for a head cold?

No eggs
No refined sugar
No milk (optional)
No wheat or cornstarch thickeners
No spices

No-Nonsense Apricot Mousse

11 ounces dried apricots
Water to cover plus ½ cup water
¼ cup orange juice concentrate
6 tablespoons agar flakes
¼ cup honey
Juice of 1 lemon
1 teaspoon grated lemon peel
2½ cups stiffly whipped heavy cream

1. Place apricots in pan with enough water to cover. Bring to boil, reduce heat, and allow apricots to simmer in water until soft. Puree fruit with water used for cooking them and orange juice concentrate.

2. Dissolve agar in the ½ cup water by boiling them together for 5 minutes.

3. In a bowl, combine dissolved agar (gelatin) liquid with 1 cup of the fruit puree and honey. Stir vigorously until smooth.

4. Add the remaining puree, lemon juice, and lemon peel. Combine the mixture thoroughly. Cool to room temperature.

5. Fold in whipped cream. Pour mousse into a 2-quart soufflé dish with waxed paper collar attached. Chill about 1 hour until mousse is firm. Serve immediately.

Options: 1. Oranges off your dessert menu? Use ½ cup Apple Fructose (see p. 86) and omit concentrate and honey. Instead of dried apricots, use dried apples. 2. Substitute a milk-free whipped topping (see Toppings and Dessert Sauces) for dairy whipped cream.

Makes 10 servings; 175 calories each

Did you know that apricots are a valuable source of vitamin A? But if they're too brightly colored they've been treated with sulfur.

Whipped Desserts

No refined sugar
No egg yolks
No wheat
No milk
No corn
No citrus
No soy
No nuts

Applesauce Soufflé

1½ cups unsweetened applesauce
1 tablespoon honey
½ teaspoon cinnamon (plus more for sprinkling on top)
3 egg whites

1. Preheat oven to 350°F.

2. Blend applesauce with honey and cinnamon in a bowl. Spoon 1 tablespoon applesauce into bottom of each of four 6-ounce custard cups.

3. In another bowl beat egg whites until stiff, but not dry. Fold half into remaining applesauce and blend well. Fold remaining whites into applesauce very gently. Spoon into custard cups. Sprinkle with cinnamon.

4. Bake about 15 to 20 minutes, until puffed and browned. Serve immediately.

Options: 1. Substitute pear sauce for applesauce. 2. Use Apple Fructose (see p. 86) in place of honey. 3. Omit cinnamon and try ½ teaspoon dried woodruff.

Makes 4 servings; 60 calories each

Did you know that the modified food starch used in commercial fruit sauces and canned fruit desserts is an alkali called sodium hydroxide which may cause lung damage and vomiting? It's on the FDA top priority list as needing further study. It is also used in drink powders and pie fillings.

No refined sugar
No citrus
No milk
No spices
No corn
No wheat

White Jello

1 bar kanten (see Note)
1½ cups cold water
1½ cups white grape juice
¾ cup seedless green grapes

1. Break kanten in pieces and soak in water for 10 minutes.

2. Place mixture in saucepan and bring to a boil, stirring, until dissolved.

3. Add juice and grapes.

4. Simmer 10 minutes. Pour into serving dishes.

5. Refrigerate until firm.

Note: Kanten is agar, a gelatin derived from seaweed (see chapter II).

Options: 1. For yellow jello, use orange juice or peach nectar in place of grape juice. 2. Substitute an allowed fruit for grapes.

Makes 2 to 3 servings; 65 calories each

Did you know that agar contains 6.3 milligrams of iron per 100 grams, 50 percent more than spinach? And it's five times richer in calcium.

Ice Cream and Ices

Ice Cream

No chocolate
No eggs
No milk
No refined sugar
No corn
No wheat
No spices

Hypoallergenic Ice Cream

5 pitted dates
½ cup raw cashews
2 tablespoons carob powder
¾ cup water
4 or 5 ripe bananas, frozen and chopped

1. Blend all ingredients except bananas in blender.

2. Slowly add the bananas.

3. When ingredients are thoroughly combined, pour into ice cube tray and freeze until firm. Or eat at once as a soft ice cream.

Options: 1. For strawberry version use 1 cup frozen strawberries and omit bananas. 2. Use figs instead of dates. 3. Try ½ cup walnuts in place of cashews.

Makes 4 small servings; 110 calories each

Did you know strawberries contain two-thirds as much stress-fighting vitamin C as oranges?

No refined sugar
No milk
No citrus
No eggs
No soy
No nuts
No spices

Icy Fingers (No-Milk Creamsicles)

½ cup dried figs
Boiling water
1 small apple, diced
1 banana, sliced
½ cup strawberries

1. Soak dried figs overnight in boiling water to cover.

2. The next day add figs and their soaking water to blender and blend with apple, banana, and strawberries.

3. Pour into Popsicle molds, or spoon into paper cups and when half-frozen insert plastic spoons.

4. Freeze until firm, remove cups and eat them like Popsicles.

Options: 1. Substitute other dried fruit for figs. 2. Use 2 bananas, omit berries. 3. For High-C Icy Fingers, soak figs in rose hip tea or add 1 teaspoon powdered ascorbic acid after blending.

Makes 6 "pops"; about 150 calories each

Did you know there are about 750 milligrams of vitamin C in 1 tablespoon of pure rose hips powder?

No eggs
No soy
No refined sugar
No citrus
No spices
No yeast

Ice Milk Muffins

½ cup nonfat dry milk
½ cup ice water
4 tablespoons Plain Grain Sugar
½ teaspoon almond extract
4 tablespoons ground almonds

1. In a bowl beat milk powder and ice water until stiff, about 7 minutes.

2. Add "sugar" and almond extract; beat in well.

3. Fold in ground almonds.

4. Line muffin tin with paper baking cups. Spoon mixture into cups. Freeze about 3 or 4 hours, until firm.

Options: 1. Use vanilla extract and finely chopped walnuts instead of almond extract and almonds. 2. For a "streusel-y" effect mix 1 teaspoon maple sugar with 1 teaspoon date sugar. Sprinkle over top of each cup before freezing.

Makes 10 small muffins; 65 calories each

Did you know that almonds raise the blood sugar better than sugar? A quarter cup contains over 6 grams of protein and 20 grams of energizing fat.

No milk
No eggs
No corn
No wheat
No soy
No spices
No refined sugar
No citrus

Confetti Snow Cones

1½ cups each of any 3 unsweetened fruit juices (such as apple, cranberry, grape)

1. Freeze each juice in a separate ice cube tray.

2. Crush the cubes one tray at a time (so as not to combine the various flavors in one) and then mix them together. Use an ice crusher, blender, or food processor.

3. Spoon into cone-shaped paper coffee cups (the kind used with holders) to create a "rainbow" effect. Serve.

Options: 1. Make Apple Fructose (p. 86) or Fig Fructose (p. 86) Snow Cones by substituting 4 cups of one of these sweeteners for the fruit juices. 2. Add crushed berries and/or a whipped milk-free topping (see Toppings and Dessert Sauces).

Makes 8 to 10 cones; 50 calories each

Did you know that drinking juices helps you fight allergic cravings? According to nutritionist Raymond LeBlanc, juices help most people control their appetites. As little as 4 ounces of orange, apple, grapefruit, or tomato juice may do the trick.

Ices

No refined sugar
No citrus
No milk
No eggs
No spices

Non-Italian Ice

2 cups unsweetened grape juice, or 1 cup cranberry juice and 1
  cup grape juice
20 cracked ice cubes

1. Prepare 2 servings at a time. In a blender or food processor process 1 cup juice and 10 ice cubes until slushy. Pour into chilled cups.

2. Repeat process with remaining juice and ice cubes and serve immediately.

Options: 1. For a sweeter version, substitute 1 cup Apple Fructose (p. 86) for 1 cup straight grape juice. 2. Add 1 teaspoon rose water or garnish with homemade Candied Violets.

Makes 4 servings; 50 to 65 calories each

Did you know that grapes are four times higher in carbohydrates than beets and a good source of energy because they are almost entirely fructose and glucose, the two sugars most readily assimilated by the body?

No refined sugar
No citrus
No milk
No nuts
No wheat
No spices

Mock Lime Sherbet

4 avocados, halved and peeled
2 tablespoons pineapple juice concentrate
1 16-ounce can crushed pineapple, packed in juice (undrained)
1 tablespoon arrowroot or cornstarch

1. In a bowl, mash ripe avocados with pineapple juice concentrate. Cover and place in freezer until frozen, about 2 hours.

2. Remove from freezer and thaw for 10 minutes.

3. Meanwhile, heat pineapple in its juice with cornstarch, stirring until thickened.

4. Remove from heat and let cool completely. Puree avocado and pineapple mixtures together in an electric blender or food processor until smooth.

5. Spoon into dessert dishes. Add topping (see Toppings and Dessert Sauces).

Options: 1. Beat 4 tablespoons whipped cottage cheese or pureed tofu into sherbet for creamier dessert. 2. Add ½ teaspoon dried mint leaves. 3. Spoon into a 2-Ingredient Piecrust (see pp. 121–124). Serve this as a sherbet pie for a sultry summer night.

Makes 6 to 7 servings; 60 calories each without topping

Want a sugarfree lift? A 500 milligram tablet of the amino acid tyrosine raises adrenaline better than sugary sherbet. Other good food sources of this protein stimulant are milk and whole-wheat bread.

Miscellaneous Fruit and Vegetable Desserts

Fruit Desserts

No corn
No soy
No refined sugar
No milk
No spices

Clockwork Oranges

4 medium-size seedless oranges, peeled
2 teaspoons maple syrup
4 teaspoons toasted chopped walnuts

1. Slice oranges, and arrange on plate in clockwise fashion, overlapping the slices.

2. In a saucepan heat syrup until warm.

3. Sprinkle orange slices with nuts. Spoon on syrup.

Options: 1. Substitute ripe diced nectarines for oranges. 2. Substitute stir-fried wheat berry sprouts (available at health food stores or do it yourself) for walnuts. 3. Serve cold with any milk-free whipped topping (see Toppings and Dessert Sauces).

Makes 4 servings; 80 calories each

Did you know that the way you eat oranges can reveal your personality? According to Barbara Burris of the citrus fruit organization called Outspan, such is the case. Biters—people who cut an orange in halves or quarters and bite out the insides—are vigorous, impatient, and very competitive. Chewers—people who don't peel first, but rip away the skin in hunks and chew out the meat—are more mature and well-balanced than average. Suckers—people who cut the orange into either halves or quarters and suck all the juices out—are very sensitive and crave security.

No refined sugar
No corn
No spices
No eggs
No milk

Spirited Fruits

This can be served as a low-calorie alternative to more mundane stewed fruits.

Oranges, strawberries, peaches in orange liqueur or
Apples in calvados
Pears in kirsch
Raspberries in framboise
Purple plums in plum brandy

1. Cube or dice any two or three fresh fruits.

2. Marinate separately in a compatible tolerated liqueur for at least 4 hours.

3. Drain well. Serve over cereal, yogurt, or ice cream.

No citrus (optional)
No spices
No wheat
No refined sugar
No milk
No nuts

Salicylate-Free Fruit Salad

A good diet lunch, or a healthy brunch. Cantaloupes are rich in vitamin A and C and lower in calories than apples, oranges, or grapes.

1 medium cantaloupe, chilled
2 cups chilled fresh mango cubes
Crisp lettuce
Plain yogurt

1. Cut cantaloupe in wedges, scoop out seeds and fiber, and pare off rind.

2. Wash and drain mango cubes.

3. Arrange melon wedges on lettuce, fill center with cubes. Top with plain yogurt.

Options: 1. Top with any milk-free whipped topping (see Toppings and Dessert Sauces) in place of yogurt. 2. Add ½ teaspoon blackstrap molasses to yogurt for high-potassium, low-calorie mock chocolate topping. 3. Substitute papaya cubes for mango.

Makes 5 servings; 60 calories each with yogurt

Did you know that salicylate-containing foods are often a contributing factor in hyperactive behavior? According to the late Dr. Benjamin Feingold, sources include almonds, apples, apricots, blackberries, cherries, cloves, cucumbers, pickles, currants, gooseberries, grapes and raisins, nectarines, oranges, peaches, plums and prunes, raspberries, and strawberries.

No wheat
No citrus
No corn
No spices
No refined sugar
No milk
No soy

Fruit Kabobs with Strawberry Dip

Kabobs:

12 (1 cup) fresh strawberries or watermelon balls
12 (1 cup) fresh pineapple chunks
½ honeydew melon

Dip:

½ cup fresh or frozen unsweetened strawberries
½ cup plain low-fat yogurt
1 teaspoon honey

1. Place strawberries or watermelon balls and pineapple chunks on toothpicks.

2. Make the dip by combining ½ cup strawberries with yogurt and honey in blender. Whirl until smooth.

3. Use ½ honeydew melon as serving dish. Place fruit kabobs around cut edge and fill center with strawberry dip.

Options: 1. Use quartered papaya or mango in place of pineapple. 2. Substitute pureed tofu for yogurt. 3. To serve as a hot dessert melt 1 tablespoon butter. Brush kabobs. Broil 5 minutes, turning twice. Roll in wheat germ while hot. Serve warm with dip.

Makes 4 servings; 50 calories each

No eggs
No milk
No wheat
No citrus
No refined sugar
No corn

Pot-Bellied Apples

5 Rome or Golden Delicious apples
1½ tablespoons sesame butter
¼ cup raisins
1 tablespoon sweet miso
3 tablespoons date sugar or maple syrup granules
2 tablespoons water
1 tablespoon lemon juice or water
¼ teaspoon cinnamon

1. Preheat oven to 350°F. Core apples halfway down.

2. Mix the remaining ingredients together in a bowl, then pack mixture firmly into hollow of each apple.

3. Wrap apples individually in foil, place on a cookie sheet, and bake for about 30 minutes. Serve hot or cold.

Options: 1. Use honey in place of miso. 2. Use any dried fruit in place of raisins. 3. Try ½ teaspoon chamomile tea herbs in place of cinnamon. 4. Substitute large pears for apples.

Makes 5 servings; 150 calories each

Did you know that Rome and Golden Delicious are the best baking apples? They also retain their shape when cooked tender. And did you know that apples are on the list of least allergenic foods? And that gymnast Olga Korbut eats five a day as energizers?

No refined sugar
No wheat
No nuts
No milk
No soy
No corn
No citrus
No spices

Water-Baked Bananas

Serve these bananas as a dessert-course vegetable with butter and herbs or sprinkle with a little date sugar and a handful of sweet sprouts.
2 medium-size firm but ripe bananas
Water as needed

1. Preheat oven to 350°F.

2. Peel fruit, slice in half vertically.

3.Place fruit in a pan with enough water to just cover the bottom.

4. Bake for 20 to 30 minutes, until fruit is easily pierced with a fork.

Options: 1. Use herb tea instead of water. 2. Bake in orange juice or Simple Honey Syrup (see p. 88). 3. Banana intolerant? Try plantains—large tropical banana-type fruits available at good greengrocers.

Makes 2 servings; 90 calories each

Did you know that the cultivated banana is the largest plant on earth without a woody stem and has a higher mineral content than any other soft fruit except the strawberry? So says the North American Vegetarian Society.

No refined sugar
No corn
No yeast
No eggs
No milk
No soy

Dessert Stir-Fries (Stir-Fried Sprouts and Fruit)

Any permitted nut or vegetable oil
2 cups sprouted wheat berries (see Options)
1 large apple, cored, peeled, and shredded
Sunflower seeds
Spices to taste (see Dessert Sprinkles, p. 83)

1. Preheat wok or skillet. Place a small amount of oil in it.

2. Add sprouted wheat and stir-fry 3 to 4 minutes. Add fruit and stir-fry another few minutes until soft.

3. Add seeds and spices and serve.

Options: 1. Steam berries before stir-frying for a softer, chewier dessert. 2. Substitute sprouted rye, rice, or oats for wheat. Available at health food stores or do it yourself. 3. Substitute shredded pear or papaya for apple.

Makes 4 to 5 servings; 100 calories each

Did you know that indigestion and food intolerance go together? Food allergies often arise when undigested food particles get into the bloodstream, and that occurs when there are weak areas in the mucous membrane of your intestines. What helps? Digestive enzymes and HCL (hydrochloric acid) supplements with every meal. Three more detoxification tips from authority Earl Irons: Don't mix heavy proteins and starches at the same meal; eliminate all refined sugars and starches; add vitamin C complex to the ascorbic acid you are using and emulsified vitamin A-E complex to your other supplements.

No chocolate
No refined sugar
No corn
No citrus
No wheat
No soy

Carob Kiwis

1 tablespoon butter
1 kiwi
Cinnamon
4 small pieces of sugar-free carob from a bar or block

1. Melt butter in a skillet. Peel kiwi and slice; place in skillet.

2. Sprinkle with cinnamon.

3. Sauté 1 minute, turn. Place pieces of carob over each slice. Cook, covered, until carob melts. Spread melted carob over fruit and serve when cooled.

Options: 1. Substitute bananas for kiwi. 2. Try nutmeg or allspice in place of cinnamon. 3. Garnish with Candied Violets (see p. 155).

Makes 1 serving; 65 calories

Did you know that any picked-too-soon-to-ripen fruit can be diced and used as a mock "vegetable" in tossed salads? Its sour taste adds a novel counterpoint to the other ingredients.

Vegetable Desserts

No refined sugar
No wheat
No corn
No citrus
No soy

Beet Sweet (The baked apple alternative)

1 medium beet
Safflower oil

1. Preheat oven to 400°F.

2. Wash beet and pat dry with a paper towel. Rub beet with a little safflower oil.

3. Place in a baking dish and bake for about 1 hour or until tender.

4. Serve like baked apple with sour cream or a sour cream substitute or top with Dessert Sprinkles (see p. 83).

Options: 1. Cut in half while hot and eat as you would a baked potato. 2. Sprinkle with stir-fried wheat sprouts (available at health food stores or make yourself) to add minerals and B vitamins. 3. Chill and eat with yogurt for a midnight snack.

Makes 1 serving; 25 calories

Did you know if you are allergic to apples, baking a beet is the best substitute? Beets are naturally sweet and baking makes them sweeter yet. Better yet, they're low in calories, and high in red blood corpuscle-building power.

No soy
No eggs
No wheat
No corn
No milk
No refined sugar

Sweet and Sour Sweets (Fruit-Vegetable Medley)

4–6 medium carrots
Boiling water to cover
2½ tablespoons sweet butter
2 teaspoons homemade sugar (see pp. 79–84) or maple syrup
  granules
½ cup pitted and chopped fresh blue plums
1 teaspoon finely slivered orange peel
1½ teaspoons lemon juice
1 teaspoon freshly ground pepper
Chopped parsley (optional)

1. Peel and trim carrots. Cut into strips 3 inches long and about ¼ inch thick. Cook in boiling water until crisp-tender, 3 to 4 minutes. Rinse under cold water, drain.

2. Melt 2 tablespoons butter in a medium-size skillet over medium heat. Add carrots, sprinkle with "sugar." Cook, tossing gently, until carrots begin to caramelize.

3. Add plums and orange peel to carrots. Cook over medium-low heat until plums give off their juice and are almost tender, about 5 minutes.

4. Stir in lemon juice and remaining butter. Raise heat slightly and cook, tossing constantly, until most of liquid has been absorbed. Add fresh pepper to taste.

5. Serve sprinkled with chopped parsley (optional).

Options: 1. Use cherries instead of plums. Try jicama in place of carrots. Good greengrocers, health food stores, and food co-ops carry jicama, a Mexican root vegetable. It's the size of a rutabaga with a taste that's a cross between an apple and a water chestnut; it can be used as you would a potato. Good raw, baked, or steamed. 2. Use peanut oil in place of butter.

Makes 4 servings; 75 calories each

Did you know pepper works as a flavor enhancer in desserts?

No refined sugar
No wheat
No corn
No eggs
No milk
No spices

Dessert Dim Sum

8 cakes fresh tofu
Arrowroot powder
1 cup Vegetable Fructose Paste (see p. 00) for filling
3–4 tablespoons peanut oil

1. Place tofu in a strainer and press gently with paper towels to extract moisture. Let drain 1 to 2 hours.

2. Cut each cake in half diagonally. With pointed knife cut out a pocket in each half of the tofu cake.

3. Dust the pocket with arrowroot, fill with 1 tablespoon of Fructose Paste filling. Pack smoothly with a knife.

4. Cook in any of the following ways: (a) Steam 8 to 10 minutes in a tightly covered bamboo or collapsible steamer over boiling water. Serve immediately. (b) Pour 2 to 3 tablespoons peanut oil in cast-iron frying pan. Heat over high flame until a wisp of white smoke appears. With stuffed side of tofu down, pan-fry over medium heat for 5 minutes. Turn cakes and cook other side for 2 minutes. Serve hot. (c) Deep-fry 2 or 3 tofu cakes at a time, in oil heated to 325°F, until each is golden brown. Drain and serve with cold spiced yogurt or Un-Yogurt (see p. 162).

Options: 1. Substitute any homemade jam in place of Fructose Paste or use 2 very ripe mashed bananas plus 1 tablespoon coarse-grained wheat germ or corn germ, to bind. 2. Use any allowed oil in place of peanut oil.

Makes 16 dim sum; 75 calories each

Did you know that 8 ounces of plain tofu supply only 147 calories and 25 percent of your daily protein requirement? After bean sprouts, tofu has the lowest ratio of calories to protein of any known plant food.

Toppings and Dessert Sauces

Toppings

No milk (optional)
No refined sugar
No spices
No corn
No wheat
No soy

Banana "Ready Whip"

1 egg white
1 sliced ripe banana

1. In a bowl beat egg white until stiff.

2. Add banana slices. Beat until banana dissolves and topping is stiff.

Options: 1. Substitute ¼ cup instant or noninstant powdered milk for banana. For stiffer cream, add more powder. 2. Add ¼ teaspoon vanilla or almond extract.

Makes 1 cup; 10 calories per heaping tablespoon

No milk
No refined sugar
No corn
No wheat
No eggs
No soy
No citrus
No spices

Cashew "Ready Whip"

Serve over any dessert or spoon on plain yogurt or cottage cheese.

2 yellow Delicious or MacIntosh apples
½–1 cup water
1 cup raw cashews

1. Core, peel, and dice apples. Turn on blender and then add apples alternately with ½ cup water.

2. Slowly add cashews and additional water if needed. Mixture should blend smoothly.

3. Blend for several minutes until you have smooth cream.

Options: 1. Use Brazil nuts instead of cashews. 2. Use chamomile or lemon mint tea in place of water.

Makes 30 tablespoons; 45 calories per tablespoon

No eggs
No corn
No milk (optional)
No soy (optional)
No refined sugar
No spices
No citrus

Three Quick Whipped Toppings

Soy-free:

½ cup instant nonfat dry milk
¼ cup ice cold water
1 teaspoon vanilla
1 teaspoon Plain Grain Sugar (optional) (see p. 79)

1. In a chilled metal bowl combine milk and water.

2. Beat with electric mixer for 3 to 4 minutes. Add vanilla and continue beating until stiff peaks form. For a sweeter version, sprinkle in "sugar."

Makes about 2/3 cup; 10 calories per tablespoon

Milk-Free:

½ teaspoon gelatin
1 tablespoon hot water
1 tablespoon soy milk powder
¼ cup cold water
¼ teaspoon lemon juice
¼ teaspoon vanilla
1 teaspoon or more honey

1. In a bowl dissolve gelatin in hot water. Stir in other ingredients.

2. Beat with electric mixer at high speed until soft peaks form.

Makes 1 cup; about 10 calories per tablespoon

Egg-Free:

12 ounces tofu
2 tablespoons honey
½ teaspoon vanilla extract (optional)

Combine all ingredients in a blender and puree until smooth.

Makes 2/3 cup; 12 calories per tablespoon

Dessert Sauces

No refined sugar
No corn
No citrus
No soy
No wheat
No milk

Peach Sauce Plus

Good over slices of a warm soufflé or cold cake.

*1 pound (about 5 to 6 small) fresh peaches, peeled, pitted, and
    chopped, or 1 10-ounce frozen package, thawed and drained*
1 tablespoon pureed raspberries or sugar-free jam

Place peaches in blender or food processor with raspberries
and blend 1 minute.

Makes about 1½ cups; 35 calories per tablespoon

Did you know that it's smarter to eat sweet than drink sweet if
you're allergic? According to the noted allergist, Dr. Carleton
H. Lee of St. Joseph, Missouri, 70 percent of all hangovers are
caused by allergic reactions. To what? You guessed it. The
ingredients from which the drink is made—usually the yeast,
the fruit or a grain.

No refined sugar
No corn
No spices
No soy
No wheat

Lime Sauce Plus

Serve over fruit salad, etc.

2 tablespoons honey
2 tablespoons lime juice
1 cup plain yogurt

1. In a saucepan heat honey briefly until warm. Mix in lime
juice, then yogurt.

2. Stir vigorously until blended.

3. Chill until ready to serve.

Makes 1¼ cups; 10 calories per tablespoon

Did you know that Americans used a record-breaking 2.2 million bushels of limes in 1981 (USDA figures)? Limes supply calcium, potassium, phosphorus, and vitamin C.

Jams, Jellies, and Spreads

No refined sugar
No corn
No artificial colors
No citrus
No spices

Instant Unsweetened Cherry Preserves

1 cup pitted dried cherries (see Options)
2 tablespoons raw wheat germ
2 tablespoons unsweetened applesauce

1. Put cherries through food processor or mill (if fruit is very dry, presoak in boiling water before processing), then mix in raw wheat germ and unsweetened applesauce.

2. Refrigerate and use as a spread.

Options: 1. Use dried apples or dried mangos in place of dried cherries, available at most health food or fancy fruit stores. 2. Substitute corn germ for wheat germ. Use ½ a pureed pear in place of applesauce.

Yield—1 cup; about 60 calories per tablespoon

Raw Cranberry Marmalade

1 lb. fresh cranberries, chopped
Water to cover
3 tablespoons raw honey

1. Cook the chopped cranberries in the water just until they pop.

2. Blend in raw honey with cranberries.

3. Spoon into jam jars and refrigerate.

Options: 1. Use 3 tablespoons chopped honeycomb in place of honey. 2. Add ½ teaspoon grated orange peel.

Yield—2 cups; 50 calories per tablespoon

Did you know that cranberries were used to treat and prevent scurvy, the vitamin C deficiency disease, in colonial times?

No refined sugar
No spices
No soy
No wheat
No corn

Papaya Jelly

1 large papaya
2 small lemons

1. Peel papaya, remove seeds.

2. Liquefy whole fruit in blender. Add the juice of 1 lemon for each 2 cups of fruit.

3. Refrigerate. Jelly will jell in a few hours.

4. Spoon into sterilized jars. Refrigerate.

Options: 1. Sweeten to taste with 2 teaspoons honey. 2. Papaya Plus—substitute 1 cup chopped fresh or canned, drained peaches for 1 cup papaya. This version is 50 percent sweeter.

Makes 1 cup; 10 calories per tablespoon

Did you know papayas are rich in vitamins C and A and contain only 55 nutrient-dense calories in 3½ ounces, plus an important-to-allergy-sufferers digestive enzyme called papain?

Spreads

No corn
No soy
No eggs
No wheat
No yeast
No refined sugar

Peanut Butter Plus

Use this enriched spread in place of regular peanut butter. Stuff celery stalks with it for snacks.

1/3 cup dry milk powder
1 cup natural peanut butter
2–3 tablespoons soft butter or safflower oil
3 tablespoons honey (optional)

1. In a bowl add a few drops of water to dry milk powder and stir into a smooth paste.

2. Blend paste into the peanut butter with a fork, then mix in the butter or oil and honey.

Options: 1. Add toasted oats for "crunchy" spread. 2. For a milk-free version, substitute nutritional yeast or soy granules for milk powder.

Makes 1¼ cups; about 35 calories per tablespoon

Confections

No refined sugar
No artificial flavors or colors
No corn
No wheat
No soy
No spices

Candied Violets

Use as a dessert garnish or as an exotic snack with a good champagne, or float a few in your morning tea.

½ cup honey
Violet flowers

1. Boil honey in a small saucepan until it reaches the hard brittle stage when a small amount is dropped into a cup of cold water.

2. Remove from heat, and quickly dip violets into mixture—no more than two or three at a time or they will stick together.

3. Immediately remove violets one at a time with a perforated spoon, letting excess honey run back into pan. Place on waxed paper until cool.

Options: 1. Try maple syrup in place of honey. 2. Use scented geranium leaves, nasturtium blossoms, squash blossoms, or rose petals in place of violets (ask at your florist if you don't grow your own).

8 calories per blossom

Did you know that if your problem allergen is to pollen or to a plant pollinated by bees, a homeopathic remedy called Apis mei (available at health food stores) may help?

No refined sugar
No corn
No spices

Vermont Candied Ginger

*1 small ginger root, cut into paper thin slices (peeled or
    unpeeled)*
1 egg white
1 teaspoon lemon juice
¼ cup maple syrup granules, or as needed

1. Dry sliced ginger with paper towel.

2. In a bowl beat egg white and lemon juice together. Dip
ginger slices in egg white wash.

3. Dredge in maple syrup granules.

4. Let slices dry at room temperature for at least 24 hours.

5. Store in airtight glass jar.

Options: 1. Substitute maple sugar for granules. 2. Grind candied ginger into a natural sugar (see recipe for Ginger Sugar, p. 83).

Makes 1/3 cup; 35 calories per tablespoon

Did you know that ginger is used by herbalists to improve digestion, hasten menstruation, soothe nerves, and remedy nausea?

No refined sugar
No chocolate
No eggs
No corn
No spices
No citrus

Brownie Buttons (Sprouted Wheat Candy)

1 cup wheat sprouts (see Note)
1 tablespoon carob powder
1 cup cream cheese
2-1/3 cups ground nuts (any nuts permitted)
Toasted wheat germ and carob powder (for dusting)

1. Blend sprouts, carob powder, and cream cheese together in a bowl.

2. With a teaspoon or your fingers, shape into 3 dozen round "buttons." Place on cookie sheet.

3. Roll in wheat germ and carob. Chill until firm.

Options: 1. Substitute corn germ or rice bran for wheat germ. 2. Instead of buttons, press into cake dish. Chill. Cut into "candy bars."

Makes 3 dozen buttons; 20 calories each

Did you know that according to Dr. Tsuneo Kada, a mutation specialist at the National Institute of Genetics in Japan, certain foods counteract nitrosamines, a potent carcinogen? And that among them are wheat sprouts? So are pumpkins and peas.

Note: Wheat sprouts are available at health food stores, or sprout your own.

No refined sugar
No milk
No corn
No spices

Sugar Cubes

2 sticks or bars of agar
2 cups warm water
¼ cup honey

1. Cut agar into 1-inch cubes and place in water to cover in saucepan.

2. Simmer lightly 20 minutes in water.

3. Drain. Press out excess liquid.

4. Put cubes in bowl. In a saucepan heat honey until hot. Pour over cubes until well coated.

5. Chill cubes 30 minutes. Sprinkle with Dessert Sprinkles (see p. 83) or lecithin granules. Or serve with a homemade whipped topping (see Toppings and Dessert Sauces) or on top of plain cottage cheese.

Options: 1. Puree and use as a syrup over ice cream, plain cakes, and yogurt. 2. For Spearmint Sugar Cubes use 2 cups spearmint tea in place of water. 3. For New England–Style Sugar Cubes use ¼ cup maple syrup instead of honey.

Makes 8 cubes; 50 calories each

Did you know that if you're avoiding wheat you have to avoid processed cheese and flavored cottage cheese? Both contain wheat as a stabilizer.

No wheat
No soy
No corn
No chocolate
No milk
No refined sugar (optional)
No spices

Carob-Dipped Orange Peel

*6 ounces sugar-free carob chips or carob grated from block or
bar*
1 pound organic orange peel strips

1. In the top of a double boiler melt carob over hot, not boiling, water.

2. Dip each strip of orange peel in carob, covering ½ to 2/3 of each piece. Shake off excess carob and lay on wax paper.

3. Cool until set and not sticky. Or let "dry" in refrigerator.

Options: 1. Substitute organic lemon peel for orange strips. 2. Use fresh or dried pitted cherries to make carob-covered cherries. 3. Add 1 tablespoon honey for a sweeter version. Or 1 tablespoon chia or poppy seed for a crunchy version.

Makes 60 strips; 6 calories each

Did you know that an organic orange is better than a supermarket orange? A supermarket orange is likely to be treated with artificial colors and hazardous chemicals, including ethylene gas used to ripen nonorganic green fruit. Residues should be within legal tolerance but may not be within your tolerance. So play it safe.

No refined sugar
No soy
No corn
No chocolate
No spices
No eggs
No citrus

Feast of Yeast Fudge

¼ cup peanut butter
¼ cup honey
2 tablespoons nutritional yeast
1 tablespoon carob powder
2–3 tablespoons instant nonfat dry milk powder

1. In a bowl mix all ingredients together well.

2. Shape into candy bars or balls.

3. Roll in any desired Dessert Sprinkles (see p. 83). Chill.

Options: 1. Use wheat germ or corn germ in place of nutritional yeast. Both supply large amounts of energizing B-complex vitamins. 2. Omit honey. Use ¼ cup maple syrup. 3. Coat in maple syrup granules or date sugar.

Makes 1 dozen balls or bars; 15 calories each

Did you know 50 percent of all U.S. households eat dessert, according to a recent *Ladies' Home Journal* survey.

No refined sugar
No corn
No wheat
No spices

Ringers

A chewy candy or candied apple substitute.

2 large ripe apples (any variety), cored and peeled
Orange or lemon juice to cover

1. Cut apples into papery-thin slices and place in a bowl. Steep in the juice for 1 hour.

2. Drain slices, pat dry, and arrange on a string or clothesline.

3. Suspend your "fruit-loop" strings in a closet or any non-humid dark room (drying triples the natural sugar content). Ready to eat in 7 to 14 days.

Options: 1. Steep sliced apples in a solution of water and powdered vitamin C if you're allergic to citrus. 2. Substitute pears for apples.

Makes about 40 ringers; 10 calories each

Did you know that apples contain potash; lime; magnesium; iron salts; mallic, gallic, and tartaric acids which neutralize the acid products of indigestion by chemically changing stomach acids to alkaline carbohydrates? In other words, apples help you digest other foods.

No refined sugar
No soy
No wheat
No corn
No added colors
No spices
No citrus
No milk

Raspberry "Chewing Gum"

Chew as a gum substitute or eat as a candy alternative.

4 quarts raspberries
1 apple, cored, peeled, and diced
2/3 cup Simple Honey Syrup (see p. 88)

1. Wash berries. Combine with apple and syrup in a blender container and puree until you have an apple-butter-like consistency.

2. Line a cookie sheet with plastic wrap. Spread pureed fruit over wrap. Set cookie sheet in a very low oven (pilot light of a gas oven or lowest setting on electric oven) until dry.

3. When fruit leather is dry (24 to 48 hours) peel off sheet and roll up.

4. Freeze. Break into "sticks."

Options: 1. Substitute blackberries or blueberries for raspberries. Or replace 1 cup berries with 1 cup any dried fruit. 2. Omit freezing. Slice into strips after rolling. Wrap individually to pack as lunch-box or brown-bag dessert.

Makes about 48 sticks of fruit gum; 10 calories each

Miscellaneous Snacks

No refined sugar
No wheat
No corn
No soy
No spices
No citrus
No milk

Yogurt

Un-Yogurt

½ cup rolled oats
Water to cover
4 tablespoons chia or sesame seed
¼ cup shredded coconut (omit for a less-sweet version)
1 teaspoon flaxseed
1 tablespoon carob powder

1. In a bowl combine all ingredients. Stir in warm water to cover.

2. "Culture" the mixture for 24 hours, like yogurt, in a warm spot, such as the top of a refrigerator or a closet.

3. After 24 hours mixture will have a tart yogurt-y flavor and texture. The longer it sits, the sharper and more pungent the flavor becomes.

Options: 1. Substitute another cereal flake, such as rye, soy, or rice, available at health food stores. 2. To reduce sweetness, omit coconut and let yogurt culture an additional 12 to 24 hours.

Makes four 6-ounce servings; 75 calories each

Did you know that although many chemically sensitive people are allergic to Teflon, tin can lining, and plastic food wrap, there are no recorded cases of allergy to glass?

Chips

Banana Ruffles

A potato chip substitute.

4 unripe bananas or 2 green plantains (a Puerto Rican fruitlike
vegetable that resembles a giant banana)
Vegetable oil (any kind tolerated)

1. Peel fruit and cut into thin slices. Place on cookie sheet.

2. Brush with oil, then broil.

3. Mash flatter with the tines of a fork to "ruffle," and broil again quickly, just until crisp.

Note: Broiling increases the natural sweetness of fruits.

Options: 1. Make Piña Colada Chips by adding a few drops of pineapple juice and a sprinkle of coconut before mashing and rebroiling. 2. To increase B-complex vitamins add ½ tea-spoon wheat germ or corn germ flakes before mashing and re-broiling.

Makes 36 chips; 8 calories each

Peanuts

No nuts
No hydrogenated fats
No salt
No sugar

Pseudo Peanuts

1 cup dried chick-peas
3 cups water
2 tablespoons any permitted vegetable oil
Wheat germ or brewers' yeast

1. Place chick-peas in a pot with water, and bring them to a boil for 2 minutes. Remove from heat and let stand at room temperature for 1 hour.

2. Preheat oven to 350°F.

3. Drain chick-peas and spread on absorbent paper to dry.

4. Spread in a shallow baking pan, sprinkle with oil, and shake until coated.

5. Bake for 1 hour until lightly browned, shaking pan oc-casionally.

6. Dry on absorbent paper, shake with wheat germ or yeast in a paper bag, and serve in a snack bowl.

Options: 1. Use other dried beans in place of chick-peas. 2. Try hazelnut oil instead of your usual lubricant for a flavor treat. 3. Boil beans in a pungent tea, such as jasmine or lemon mint, instead of water.

Makes 2½ cups; 150 calories per ¼ cup

Did you know that if allergy is present on one side of your family, you have a 50 percent chance of developing an allergy to something at some time in your life? And if allergy is present on *both* sides of the family, your chances of becoming allergic rise to 75 percent?

10 Instant Gratifications

1. Confetti punch: Pour different unsweetened fruit juices into ice cube trays. Freeze. Float in punch bowl of lemonade, or use as individual juice bracers.
2. Quick unchocolate chip ice cream: Chop up one 4 ounce plain or nut-flavored carob bar. Add to softened vanilla ice cream. Refreeze.
3. Confectionary craving? Stuff a plate of dates with peanut butter spiked with a trace of grated horseradish.
4. Instant poppy-seed spread: Grind dry poppy seed and stir into blender-pureed raisins. Raisins should be soaked in warm water until plump before putting in blender.
5. Strawberries are a very good source of vitamin C. Gram for gram, they contain a little more vitamin C than oranges or orange juice. Strawberries pureed in a blender make a nice topping on yogurt or whole-wheat pancakes. This puree can be made in larger quantities and frozen in freezer containers.
6. Mix a teaspoon of bee pollen in a glass of spring water in the morning. Use as a base for blender drinks or simply drink as-is with vitamins.

7. Add carob powder to Tofu "Half and Half" for a failure-proof mock chocolate mousse. Or add lemon juice and honey to the cream substitute to make a smooth lemon custard without cooking.

8. Make your own mint toothpicks. Soak plain toothpicks in slightly diluted oil of peppermint or peppermint extract overnight. Remove from liquid and dry at room temperature. Use to serve cut pineapple.

9. An alternative to jam or jelly on toast? Spread on Health Mincemeat.

10. Coffee-cheese spread: Combine 2 tablespoons hot decaffeinated coffee or hot Postum with 3 ounces of cream cheese. Fork-whip until smooth; spread on fruit bread or horizontally sliced raw bananas.

VI. 50 Survival Tips for the Allergic

1. How to neutralize a bad reaction to a goody? Nine out of ten times, you can take the edge off of an allergic migraine, an on-coming depression, or a topically caused upset stomach by swallowing ¼ to ½ teaspoon bicarbonate of soda or Alka-Seltzer Gold stirred into a large glass of lukewarm water. If once is not enough, the dose can safely be repeated at one or two hour intervals. Calcium ascorbate powder (vitamin C) helps, too.

2. Got highway hay fever? It could be the crop of mold in your car's air conditioner. According to Dr. Prem Kumar of the Louisiana State University School of Medicine, if you cough, wheeze, or suffer other respiratory problems whenever you drive your car, cleaning your auto air conditioner regularly may be the remedy.

3. If you're chemically sensitive, don't take dimenhydrinate (Dramamine) for seasickness or the travel woozies. New studies indicate that two capsules of old-fashioned pow-

dered ginger is twice as effective. An added benefit? Ginger doesn't make you drowsy the way Dramamine does.

4. Allergic to chemically colored and highly sugared antihistamine medications? If you can tolerate citrus, you can make your own antihistamine with built-in vitamin C. Cut untreated orange peels into strips and soak in apple cider vinegar overnight. Drain, cover with raw, unfiltered honey, and cork until honey is almost evaporated and the peels are "candied." Refrigerate. Eat a strip or two at a time to clear nasal passages. Citrus peels supply bioflavinoids, a vitamin C factor not found in commercial juices.

5. Which sweet allergens cause the *most* migraines? Milk, cheese, eggs, chocolate, tea, wheat, oranges, and apples. Migraine sufferers studied by Dr. Jean Monro of the National Hospital for Nervous Diseases in London, England, had an average of three in their diet. Eliminating them brought relief in less than two weeks.

6. Lose two pounds in five to seven days? It's possible, say allergists, if you avoid foods to which you are acutely sensitive. Why? Food allergies tend to cause fluid retention.

7. Don't get your vitamins A and B from the A&P if you're allergic. The B vitamins you're taking to cope with your allergies commonly contain large amounts of corn; brewers' yeast; and sugars derived from beets, corn, or cane. Lactose (milk sugar) is a common ingredient in homeopathic cell salts and most vitamin C is manufactured from corn unless the label tells you otherwise. Two companies that specialize in allergy-free supplements are Freeda Vitamins and Bronson Pharmaceuticals. (See Appendix B, Mail Order Sources, for addresses.)

8. Be your own allergy sleuth. Make a list of the foods you eat every day—or at least once every three days—and single out those you enjoy most. Totally eliminate them one at a time for four or more days. Then reintroduce each food unaccompanied by any of the others. If you receive a bad reaction to something, especially if it reproduces symptoms you've had in the past, it is usually

the one to which you are allergic. (For details on this self-test and others read *Dr. Mandell's Five-Day Allergy Relief System.*)

9. Sprout your favorite food and you may not have to do without it. Sprouting beans, wheat, corn, rice, and even nuts, often reduces their allergy-producing potential.

10. Stir-frying is another allergy-reducing agent, says Dr. Robert Forman in his book *How to Control Your Allergies.* "People who are only marginally sensitive to some foods may benefit from the stir-fry technique. . . . When foods are cooked quickly in a small amount of oil in a hot utensil, the oil slows down the absorption rate of the food by the body and spaces it out enough so that no reactions develop."

11. Don't use an allergen-activating mouthwash to rinse your mouth clean of allergen-free cake crumbs. *Most* commercial mouthwash preparations contain sugar, artificial colors and flavoring, plus one or more chemical preservatives and any of them may be derived from citrus, corn, wheat, sugar beet, or sugarcane. If you've gotta gargle or rinse, use lemon juice, which can neutralize harmful and infectious bacteria, combat all kinds of infections of the respiratory tract, and diluted with water and honey, makes a good astringent and a good gargle for a sore throat.

12. Ask your doctor about aromatic compound immunity therapy, called the most dramatic allergy development in twenty years. "Most food allergies are triggered by natural substances called aromatic compounds," says Dr. Robert Gardner, a Brigham Young University researcher, who has pinpointed the compounds most likely to produce allergic reactions such as cramps, diarrhea, pains in muscles and joints, and chronic fatigue. Patients fed tiny doses of the compounds to which they are allergic gradually build up an immunity to the food and become unallergic again.

13. Potatoes on the menu? Almost all restaurants buy preprocessed French fries which have been dipped in a solu-

tion of sulfur dioxide to prevent browning. (The same sulfur treatment is often applied to potato chips and even to freshly cut apples and peaches in restaurants.) Clinical ecologist Theron G. Randolph calls sulfur "a major food contaminant which can bring on mental and physical symptoms."

14. "Often the state of the food can make a difference in the allergic individual's ability to tolerate it," says Dr. Claude Frazier. "Cooked food, for example, is less likely to cause a reaction than raw food. And, oddly enough, food on the stale side is less likely to produce symptoms than very fresh food."

15. Allergen-free alternative to Ex-Lax? Try strawberry seeds (see Appendix B, Mail Order Sources). They aid constipation, say herbalists, because they are not broken down by gastric juices, and act as a stimulant to the bowels. Strawberries are high in the anti-anemia nutrient iron and their rich supply of salicylic acid aids liver and kidney functions.

16. Candy's dandy, but liquor may be quicker if you're allergic. And your favorite after-dinner drink may just be the food to which you are most allergic—in disguise. Take a look at what's in your favorite after-dinner drink. Beer contains yeast, malted barley, corn, rice, and hops, and wine has grapes (and other fruits), yeast, sugar. Brandy (and distilled wine) have fruit, sugar, caramel, and yeast; and rum contains molasses, yeast, and caramel. Egg white is used as a clarifier in beer, wine, and brandy.

17. Are the sugar blues and the stop-smoking blues one and the same? According to allergist Morton Walker, a person who has stopped smoking may eat excessively in his or her subconscious search for a new source of sugar. Smoking allows the body to absorb some sugar. Without cigarettes, a person has to eat more sugar-containing foods to replace that which is found in the tobacco smoke. Thus, his or her smoking addiction may really be an allergic addiction to sugar. A whole-food, high-protein diet helps you kick both habits.

18. Chemically sensitive? Use the right antihistamine to counteract your dessert reactions. According to the *New England Journal of Medicine,* a tranquilizerlike ingredient in some antihistamines can cause a tic, tremor, or twitch when used regularly. Check with your doctor about alternative drugs.

19. Give your body "an allergic rest period," say clinical ecologists, and in six months you should be able to eat 50 to 70 percent of the foods you can't tolerate now.

20. *Avoid* smoke, paint, insect spray, mothballs, and even felt-tipped pens. Allergic symptoms from foods are often aggravated by chemical stress.

21. Are Ring Dings your feel-good food? Any food that makes you feel more alert, more energetic, or gives you a sense of well-being is "a response that indicates food addiction," says the head of the New England Foundation for Allergic Diseases, "one of the most common factors in food allergy."

22. Are you allergic or aren't you? Write Rescue Test, a service of the Institute for Biological Ecology, Inc. (55 E. Monroe, Suite 4320, Chicago, IL 60603) to find out. Rescue Test monitors your physical and emotional reactions to suspected allergens while you actually ingest samples of them and they guarantee a "50 percent refund to any client if no relief of symptoms is recognized within three months following the tests."

23. Allergic to smoke? Buy a supply of invisible nasal filters. Most drugstores stock them.

24. Avoid restaurants that use gas—for cooking or illuminating. It often induces allergic attacks. Ditto Sterno.

25. Barbiturates and tranquilizers are poorly tolerated by the allergic. If you can't sleep, maybe you need to restore your body's mineral balance. You can do that by simmering a small head of lettuce in a pint of water (or milk, which contains nature's tranquilizer amino acid, L-tryptophan) for 15 minutes. It makes a healthy no-frills sleep potion, rich in iron, iodine, phosphorus, copper, zinc, potassium, and calcium.

26. Natural or processed? If you've got your pick, protect

your family and pick the first. According to Dr. Ray Wunderlich, a St. Petersburg, Florida, pediatrician and hyperactivity authority, "An allergic child can often eat a natural product, such as a raw, ripe organic orange, but will have an allergic reaction to orange juice, which is usually made from unripened oranges, is heated and then sits in a bottle on a shelf."

27. Taken orally one-and-a-half hours before exercise, 500 milligrams of vitamin C reduces bronchospasm in victims of exercise-induced asthma, says Dr. E. Neil Schachter of Yale University.

28. Acutely allergic to gluten? Have a banana. Banana sugars, because of their easy accessibility to the body, are useful for lessening and controlling the effects of celiac disease (gluten allergy). Bananas are also a good source of blood pressure–normalizing potassium.

29. Are you on an elimination diet that bans conventional candy bar ingredients? Look for Shiloh Farms' Powerpak containing ginseng, rose hips, cherry bark, linden flowers, and more heady healthy herbs.

30. "Sixty-five percent of all low blood sugar sufferers experience depression and symptoms of allergic reaction," says allergist H. L. Newbold. What helps? Boosting the level of vitamins B_3 and B_6. This steps up production of serotonin, a brain chemical essential to mental stability.

31. Test yourself for "psychoallergy"—a form of food sensitivity that affects the brain and nervous system. Fast for half a day. Take your pulse in a resting position every two hours to establish a base. At 2:00 P.M. record your pulse again, eat a portion of some food common in your diet. Fifteen minutes later record your pulse again. Wait three hours, consume another common food, and record your pulse fifteen minutes later. Continue this testing until you've consumed (one at a time) all the common foods you eat. A rise in pulse rate of more than ten beats per minute signifies an allergic reaction.

32. Allergylike reactions can have other causes. Here are three, according to Dr. S. Allan Bock, pediatric allergist

at the National Jewish Hospital Asthma Center in Denver:

- Sensitivity to a natural substance or a contaminant, such as penicillin in milk (from antibiotics given to cows) or red tide contamination of seafood.
- Enzyme deficiencies, such as insufficiency of lactase, the enzyme that digests the milk sugar, lactose.
- Stress and emotional problems.

33. Phenylalaline is an amino acid said to suppress allergic symptoms. It is found naturally in high proportions in spirulina, the blue-green algae sold in powder form at all health food stores. Even if it doesn't help with allergies, it lifts your energy levels. Some marathon runners have reported that the level of energy yielded by a spirulina cocktail is superior to that of "carbohydrate loading," a common runner's practice in which large quantities of starchy and sugary foods are consumed prior to a big race.

34. You can take the edge off an allergic reaction—maybe even eliminate it—by taking protein-digesting pancreatic enzymes with meals. A good supplement should provide 300 to 400 milligrams of pancreas concentrate. Half a teaspoon of sodium bicarbonate (baking soda) in a glass of water after meals also helps you prevent food reactions by raising the alkalinity of your stomach.

35. Allergy crisis? Try cysteine, an amino acid that inactivates the insulin raised by a reaction and brings blood sugar levels back to normal. One gram of cysteine helps, say nutritionists Durk Pearson and Sandy Shaw. But always take it with at least 3 grams (3,000 milligrams) of vitamin C.

36. Going cold turkey with an allergen? The best way to relieve withdrawal symptoms, advises allergist Dr. William H. Philpott, is with large doses of vitamins C, B_6, B_3, B_5 (pantothenic acid), calcium, and magnesium.

37. Too much of a good thing is a bad thing. "In 95 percent of food allergy cases," says Dr. Joseph McGovern, an adjunct professor at Brigham Young University, "the re-

action is caused by eating too much of a specific food. It is only in the remaining five percent that a person is born with an allergy, and eating patterns do not affect it."

38. A hangover may be nothing but an allergic reaction in disguise. Don't think so? Try this test: The next time instead of "hair-of-the-dog" (an additional drink of what did you in), take a bite of food made from the same fermentable food substance present in the alcoholic beverage. Eat rye toast if it was rye whiskey. Take a slice of whole-wheat bread if it was a blended whiskey. Suck some sugarcane if it was rum. Your hangover may disappear that way, and you'll recognize that you have an allergic addiction to that food.

39. Pregnant? Don't pass your allergies on. A mother who consumes large quantities of a certain food can sensitize her baby. Such newborns often develop allergic reactions the first few months after birth.

40. If you're very allergic, eat *very* few processed foods. According to FDA regulations, many ingredients do not have to be listed on a package if they appear in small enough quantities.

41. Improve your antibody production and shorten allergic suffering. Food reactions can occur immediately or one to two hours after eating, but they can last up to ten days. The faster your body's natural antibodies can react with the food allergen, the sooner you'll feel better. Supplements of vitamins E, C, A, and the trace mineral selenium are musts.

42. What allergy test is best? The most popular method, the Four-Day Fast, has a 90 percent accuracy rate. The least effective is the skin test which pinpoints food problems only 20 percent of the time.

43. Could it be cocoa beans that make you restless as a Mexican jumping bean? According to Dr. Doris Rapp, allergist at the Meyer Memorial Hospital in Buffalo, New York, tests of hyperactive children showed that over 70 percent had allergies and 50 percent improved in *one week or less* on a diet that excluded cocoa, eggs, wheat, corn, sugar, and milk.

44. Grain sensitive? Pass up vitamin E oil capsules which are usually concentrated extracts of wheat. Vitamin E is available in chewable and nonchewable dry tablets.

45. Take your amino acids. (Bee pollen, if you can tolerate it, is an excellent source of all twenty-two of these.) You may be eating these building blocks of protein in your foods but most allergy sufferers have poor pancreatic function so their bodies cannot absorb the amino acid as readily. Poorly digested proteins induce allergic responses when they pour into the blood stream. Amino acid supplementation—two to eight tablespoons a day—can improve your tolerance for both offending foods and inhalants, such as pollen and hydrocarbon fumes.

46. Are you a food-allergic traveler? Carry buffered vitamin C (it's easily tolerated and free of starch). A little bit stirred into warm water helps neutralize a food reaction. Furthermore, don't drink alcohol—it always heightens allergic symptoms.

47. Need hypoallergenic bedding, a couch without chemical fixtures, a pillow that won't make you sneeze? Call the Human Ecology Research Foundation in Dallas, Texas, (214) 620-0620.

48. Have allergic hives? Common nonfood causes include drugs, tight clothes, insect repellents, and makeup. And many sensitive sufferers even have hivelike allergic responses to summer heat, winter cold, and too much sun.

49. Help your allergic self and your fellow sufferers: $15 buys membership in the national organization HEAL (Human Ecology Action League), Suite 6506, 505 N. Lake Shore Drive, Chicago, IL 60611. There's a chapter near you.

50. Are you allergic to your house? Common allergies include dust, feathers, plastic, carpet chemicals, a moldy basement, bathroom vaporizers, mattress stuffing, and, of course, pets. If you're house allergic you'll feel worse in the colder months, at night, and upon arising.

Appendix

A. It's All in the Family: The Dessert Allergen Family Tree

Food families are groups of foods that share a similar botanical makeup. They are relatives, as it were. If one causes trouble, another family member may do the same. Knowing that carob is related to peanuts and licorice, or that cardamom is a cousin of ginger can save you needless suffering.

APPLE FAMILY
apple
   apple cider
   apple vinegar
pear
quince
ARROWROOT FAMILY
arrowroot

BANANA FAMILY
banana
plantain
BIRCH FAMILY
filbert
hazelnut
oil of birch
    wintergreen

BOVINE FAMILY
beef
butter
cheese
cow's milk
gelatin
veal
BUCKWHEAT FAMILY
buckwheat
rhubarb
sorrel
CASHEW FAMILY
cashew
mango
pistachio
CITRUS FAMILY
angostura
citron
grapefruit
kumquat
lemon
lime
orange
tangerine
    mandarin orange
FUNGI FAMILY
mushrooms
yeast
truffles
mold-containing foods
GINGER FAMILY
cardamom
ginger
turmeric
GOOSEFOOT FAMILY
beet
    beet sugar
spinach
Swiss chard
GRAINS (GRASSES)
bamboo
barley
corn
    grits
    meal
    oil
    starch
    sugar (syrup)
        dextrose
        glucose
millet
oats
rice
rye
sorghum
sugarcane
    molasses
wheat
    bran
    farina
    flour
        gluten
        graham
    germ (oil)
    semolina
    triticale
wild rice
GRAPE FAMILY
grape
    brandy
    champagne
    cream of tartar
    raisins
    vinegar
    wine

LAUREL FAMILY
avocado
cinnamon
sassafras
LEGUMES
black-eyed pea
carob
chick-pea
garbanzo bean
gum acacia
gum tragacanth
jack bean
kidney bean
lentil
licorice
lima bean
mung bean
navy bean
pea
peanut
pinto bean
soybean
 lecithin
 tofu
string bean
MAPLE FAMILY
maple sugar
maple syrup
MINT FAMILY
basil
catnip
horehound
lavender
marjoram
mint
oregano
peppermint
rosemary

sage
savory
spearmint
thyme
MISCELLANEOUS
honey
MYRTLE FAMILY
allspice
clove
guava
paprika
pimento
NUTMEG FAMILY
mace
nutmeg
ORCHID FAMILY
vanilla
PALM FAMILY
coconut
 oil
date palm
dates
sago
PHEASANT FAMILY
chicken
 chicken eggs
duck
 duck eggs
goose
 goose eggs
grouse
guinea hen
partridge
pheasant
squab
turkey
PLUM FAMILY
almond

apricot
cherry
nectarine
peach
plum
    prune
ROSE FAMILY
blackberry

boysenberry
raspberry
strawberry
STERCULIA FAMILY
cocoa
    chocolate
cola
gum karaya

B. Mail Order Sources

Can't find it at your local supermarket, health food store, or gourmet shop? Try one of the following. Catalogs available.

SOURCE	PRODUCTS
Walnut Acres Penns Creek PA 17862	Extensive stock—everything from agar gelatin substitute to unsulfured fruits, soy milks, and natural allergen-free flavoring extracts and natural food colors
Aphrodisia Products, Inc. 282 Bleecker Street New York, NY 10014	Huge stock of herbs—fresh, dried, and liquid; exotic spices and cooking ingredients
Vermont Country Maple, Inc. Jericho Center VT 05465	Pure maple syrup and maple syrup granules processed without formaldehyde or chemical additives

Springtree Corporation BX 1160 Brattleboro, VT 05301	Pure maple syrup, carob powder, carob syrup
Ener-G-Foods 6901 Fox Avenue South Seattle, WA 98124	Allergen substitutes including egg replacements, milk substitutes, cake mix substitutes, more
Fearn Soya Foods 1206 North 31st Street Melrose Park, IL 60160	Allergen substitutes, same as above
Bronson Pharmaceuticals 4526 Rinetti Lane La Canada, CA 91011	Nonallergenic vitamin supplements
Freeda Vitamins 36 East 41st Street New York, NY 10017	Algin powder, starch- and sugar-free vitamins, sugar substitutes
Jaffe Bros. Valley Center, CA 92082	Untreated dried fruits, nuts, seeds, grains, unrefined olive and sesame oils, and other natural foods
Erewhon Natural Foods 236 Washington Street Brookline, MA 02146	Complete supply of items, similar to Walnut Acres above

C. Suggested Reading

The Allergy Encyclopedia edited by the Asthma and Allergy
Foundation of America and Craig T. Norback (NAL Books,

1981); contains good shopping guide to alternative products and services.

Dr. Mandell's 5 Day Allergy Relief System by Marshall Mandell, M.D. and Lynn Waller Scanlon (Pocket Books, 1979)

If your bookstore does not carry the titles below, write Dickey Enterprises, 635 Gregory Road, Ft. Collins, CO 80524.

Allergies and the Hyperactive Child by Doris J. Rapp, M.D.

Allergy—The Great Masquerader by William Crook, M.D.

An Alternative Approach to Allergies by Theron G. Randolph, M.D. and Ralph W. Moss, Ph.D.

Basics of Food Allergy by J. C. Breneman, M.D.

Brain Allergies by William H. Philpott, M.D. and Dwight K. Kalita, Ph.D.

Coping with Your Allergies by Natalie Golos and Frances Golos
Dr. Mandell's Allergy-Free Cookbook by Fran Gare Mandell, M.S.

Don't Drink Your Milk! by Frank A. Oski, M.D. with John D. Bell

How to Control Your Allergies by Robert Forman, Ph.D.

The Sugar Primer by Beatrice Trum Hunter

Tracking Down Hidden Food Allergy by William G. Crook, M.D.

Your Child and Allergy by William G. Crook, M.D.

For further information on allergy management, all of the following supply books, pamphlets, and reprints upon request and answer questions.

Allergy Foundation of America
801 Second Avenue
New York, NY 10017

Allergy Information Association
25 Poynter Drive, Room 7
Weston, Ontario M9R 1K8
Canada

American Allergy Association
P.O. Box 7273
Menlo Park, CA 94025

HEAL
Suite 6506
505 N. Lake Shore Drive
Chicago, IL 60611

Human Ecology Research Foundation
12100 Webbs Chapel Road
Dallas, TX 75234

New England Foundation for Allergic and Environmental
Diseases
3 Brush Street
Norwalk, CT 06850

U.S. Food and Drug Administration
Consumer Communications
Room 15 B-32
5600 Fishers Lane
Rockville, MD 20852

Index